a short & happy guide to

The Law of Sales

(Contracts for the Sale of Goods)

Second Edition

Paula A. Franzese
Peter W. Rodino Professor of Law
Seton Hall Law School

Creator and Editor of the Short and Happy Guide Series

A SHORT & HAPPY GUIDE® SERIES

WEST ACADEMIC

860 Blue Gentian Road, Suite 350
Eagan, MN 55121
1-877-888-1330

Published in the United States of America

ISBN: 979-8-89209-797-0

Preface

Thank you for using this book. Thank you for choosing a career in the law. This world needs your contributions, especially now, when the promise of equal access to justice remains to be achieved for many. My wish is that you wield the instrument of the law to help to close the gap between what is and what ought to be. Continue to be a force for the good. Use your emerging expertise to give people something to believe in. Because when all is said and done, if you can do that, well, that is something to be really happy about.

Education is the great equalizer and knowledge is power. No matter the daily challenges, you are on the road to making your dreams come true. So many will never get the chance that you have now. You are creating something for your sake and for theirs, and it is very good and very important.

When you find yourself doubting your abilities and your place in the world, think about all of the hard work, sacrifice, and achievement that brought you here. We suffer because we forget. Call on the people who love you most, who believe in you and who know the song in your heart. Let them sing it to you when your memory falters. Your parents, grandparents, their parents and ancestors before them struggled and triumphed so that you would have the opportunity to be where you are at this very moment. The hard work has already been done. The table has been set. All you need to do is take your seat, respectfully and with great humility but also with the presence of mind to know that you belong here, you will thrive here, and you will use your life to bear living witness to the legacy of virtue that preceded you and the promise that awaits.

Paula A. Franzese

2026

About the Author

Professor Paula A. Franzese, the Peter W. Rodino Professor of Law at Seton Hall Law School, is one of the country's leading experts in property law as well as government ethics. She has spearheaded ethics reform initiatives on behalf of three governors, serving as Special Ethics Counsel to Governor Richard J. Codey, Chair of the State Ethics Commission, Vice-Chair of the Election Law Enforcement Commission, Vice-Chair of the New Jersey Supreme Court's Special Committee on Attorney Ethics and Admissions and as ethics advisor to state and local governments across the country, including then Mayor Cory Booker's administration in Newark. She received the National Council on Governmental Ethics Laws (COGEL) Award, the highest honor conferred by the organization, in recognition of her "significant, demonstrable and positive contributions to the fields of campaign finance, elections, ethics, freedom of information and lobbying over a significant period of time." Among her groundbreaking initiatives in those arenas, she and retired Justice Daniel J. O'Hern promulgated the Uniform Ethics Code, a pioneering statutory achievement and model for national replication. She has published extensively on the best practices for ethics reform of state and local governments.

Professor Franzese's scholarship in the area of housing law includes critical examination of landlord tenant law, common interest communities, homeowners associations and the dilemma of privatization, the law of servitudes, exclusionary zoning, affordable housing, adverse possession doctrine and takings law. Her empirical study of the plight of the working poor living in substandard housing formed the basis for significant reform efforts. She joined in the submission to the Supreme Court of an amicus brief in the *Kelo* case, and has written on takings law reform.

Professor Franzese is the creator of the *Short and Happy Guide* series and is the author of *A Short and Happy Guide to Property* (2d ed.), *A Short and Happy Guide to Being a Law Student* and *A Short and Happy Guide to Being a College Student*. She is a Fellow of the American College of Real Estate Lawyers and the American Bar Foundation as well as the recipient of numerous awards, including the St. Thomas More Medal of Honor, the YWCA Woman of Influence Award, the Women Lawyers Association Trailblazer Award, the New Jersey State Bar Foundation's Medal of Honor and the Bishop Bernard J. McQuaid Medal, Seton Hall University's highest honor.

Nationally renowned for her excellence in teaching, a book names Professor Franzese one of only 26 "best law teachers in the United States." The book, *What the Best Law Teachers Do* (Harvard University Press), profiles in detail the pedagogical approach that renders her a "dazzlingly effective model of rigor, hard work, creativity, and humility." Professor Franzese is the unprecedented ten-time recipient of the Student Bar Association's Professor of the Year Award, was named "Exemplary Teacher" by the American Association of Higher Education, was ranked the Top Law Professor in New Jersey by the New Jersey Law Journal and was named University Faculty Teacher of the Year. She has demonstrated her pedagogical expertise on teaching as both art and science at workshops and colloquia across the country.

Other *Short and Happy* Titles by Paula A. Franzese

A Short and Happy Guide to Property (2d ed.)

A Short and Happy Guide to Being a Law Student

A Short and Happy Guide to Being a College Student

Table of Contents

A Short & Happy Guide to The Law of Sales

(Contracts for the Sale of Goods)

Second Edition

"Be a force for good. Use your emerging expertise to give people hope. Because when all is said and done, if you can do that, well, that is something to be really happy about."

Paula A. Franzese

CHAPTER 1

An Introduction to Article 2 of the Uniform Commercial Code

The Law of Sales

The law of sales is contained in Article 2 of the Uniform Commercial Code ("UCC" or "Code"). The brainchild of legal realist Karl Llewellyn,[1] the UCC emerged as one of the most successful statutory achievements of the twentieth century. Its provisions on sales, or contracts for the sale of goods, aim to clarify, simplify, and modernize what previously was known as "the law merchant," or the way things were done in the marketplace of mercantile exchange.

Karl Llewellyn understood that the law must be just, and that justice is served when rigor is fused with virtue. He observed, *"Compassion without technique is a mess. But technique without compassion is a menace."*

[1] Karl Llewellyn, one of the most influential scholars of the 20th Century, was a primary drafter of the UCC. His approach to legal realism is summarized in his iconic book written for law students, The Bramble Bush: On Our Law and Its Study (1930).

As a testament to its success, Article 2 has been enacted in forty-nine states (Louisiana applies a hybrid of civil law, common law and statutory law). Moreover, even when a given transaction is outside Article 2's scope, courts have demonstrated a willingness to apply by analogy the statute's sections.

Each state's version of Article 2 will contain variations, albeit usually slight, and each state's judiciary will interpret the relevant Article 2 provisions through its own lens of perception. That is why in practice it is important to know which state's version of the UCC (and thereby which state's case law) applies to the given transaction that you are working on.

When presented with a question within the scope of Article 2, your first task will be to discern which of its provisions potentially applies to the dispute's resolution. Then, armed with those potentially relevant statutory provisions, you will be equipped to delve into the applicable jurisdiction's case law on point.

How to Organize Your Article 2 Outline and Work Product

Organize your class notes, outline and exam review into four sections: **Formation of Contract**, **Content of the Contract**, **Performance of the Contract** and **Breach of the Contract**. That order follows the same sequence used by Article 2. It makes intrinsic sense because whether on an exam or in practice, the first matter to address is whether or not a valid contract for the sale of goods has been formed. If so, the next task is to discern that contract's relevant terms. Once the contract's terms are known, it becomes important to know whether or not the parties satisfied their performance obligations in accordance with the contract's terms. If not, an examination of breach of contract must be undertaken to know which remedies are available.

In summary, since the law of sales is the product of a statute, your analysis of the subject matter should be statute-specific and organized in accordance with Article 2's own internal symmetry. To make that task easier, relevant UCC sections are included in this guide.

To recap, the four sections of analysis to use when studying contracts for the sale of goods comport with Article 2's organization. Organize your study of Article 2 into the following four sections:

(1) Formation of the contract—the 2-200s

(2) Content of the contract—the 2-300s

(3) Performance of the contract—the 2-600s

(4) Breach of the contract and remedies for breach—the 2-700s

CHAPTER 2

Getting Started: Article 2's Scope and Governing Principles

Article 2 Applies to Contracts for the Sale of Goods

Article 2 does not apply to all contracts. It applies to contracts for the sale of goods. In determining whether the given transaction is within Article 2's scope, you must ask two questions. First, is the subject matter of the deal a **"good"** as defined by § 2-105 and second, does the transaction qualify as a **"sale"** of that good as defined by § 2-106?

Defining "Goods" for Purposes of Article 2

§ 2-105: Definitions: "Goods"

> **"Goods" means all things (including specially manufactured goods) which are movable at the time of identification to the contract for sale other than the money in which the price is to be paid, investment securities (Article 8) and things in action. "Goods" also includes the unborn young of animals**

and growing crops and other identified things attached to realty as described in the section on goods to be severed from realty.

To qualify as a "good," the subject matter of the transaction must possess "tangible movability." Goods include items that you might buy from the shelves of a store or order online, such as clothing, furniture, books, groceries and appliances. Goods include moving vehicles. Goods include crops growing. Goods include fixtures, or items annexed to realty.

By contrast, real estate or land is not a good. It is not movable. Patents, trademarks and copyrights are not goods. They are not tangible, but instead intangibles.

Take the "Good or No Good" Quiz

To anchor your understanding of Article 2's definition of goods, cover the answers on the right side of the chart with your hand and read the items listed on the left side of the chart. Decide whether the given item is a good within Article 2's scope or "no good" and not within the statute's scope.

Item	"Good" or "No Good"
A car	Good—tangible and movable
A home	No Good—not movable
A customized wedding cake	Good—tangible and movable
A mobile home	Good—tangible and movable
A cemetery plot	No Good—not movable
A headstone	Good—tangible and movable
A patent	No Good—not movable
A shih-tzu	Good—animals are goods

Item	"Good" or "No Good"
Crops growing	Goods—tangible and movable no matter temporary connection to land

Defining a "Sale" of Goods

§ 2-106: Definitions: "Sale"

A sale consists in the passing of title from the seller to the buyer for a price.

To qualify as a sale, seller must transfer ownership of the good to buyer and buyer in turn must remit payment for the good. Hence, gifts of goods are not within Article 2's scope. Leases of goods and bailments are not within Article 2's scope. A bailment is the entrusting of a good to another for some limited purpose that does not include the passing of title or ownership. For example, when you take your shirts to the dry cleaner you are a party to a bailment. Article 2 does not apply when the dry cleaner damages your laundry.

Hybrid transactions involving both the sale of goods and the provision of services.

Many commercial exchanges involve both the provision of goods and services. For example, a landscaper charges for his services as well as for the shrubs he plants. Or the fee for a plumber's services might include the costs of the faucet that the plumber installed.

Article 2 does not apply to pure services contracts (such as the contract for a wedding singer). It does apply to contracts that involve both the provision of goods and services when the sale of goods represents the predominant purpose of the transaction. Many courts deem the sale of goods the predominant purpose of the transaction when their value exceeds fifty percent of the transaction's total cost. Other courts assess whether similarly situated parties would reasonably expect the contract to be primarily for goods as opposed to services, in which case Article 2 will apply.

Section 2-102 adds that, in accordance with the important norm of freedom to contract, the parties could choose to opt into Article 2 coverage even for hybrid transactions that would otherwise be excluded from Article 2's scope. Conversely, by private agreement the parties could choose to opt out of Article 2's scope even when the predominant purpose of the transaction is the sale of goods.

Time to Play "Deal or No Deal"

Cover the right side of this chart with your hand. Take a look at the transaction listed on the left side of the chart and decide whether it qualifies as a sale (*deal*) and thus within Article 2's scope or not (*no deal*).

Transaction	**Deal or No Deal**
Ross gives Rachel a watch for her birthday.	No Deal (It's a gift).
Joey brings Chandler's dog to the groomer.	No Deal (It's a bailment).
Phoebe gets a haircut.	No Deal (It's a services contract).
Christmas Décor decorates Monica's house.	Deal if sale of goods is predominant factor.
Chandler buys Broadway show tickets.	No Deal (Tickets create licenses).

The Relevance of Article 1 to Article 2 Contracts

Article 1 of the UCC contains a glossary of relevant terms and governing policies for each article of the UCC, including the law of sales. Many students and practitioners overlook Article 1 when they study and assimilate the law of sales. Do not make that mistake. Article 1 is a goldmine of salient information relevant to the law of sales. Here are the Article 1 sections to pay particular attention to.

Article 1's Guidance on How to Construe Article 2

§ 1-103: How to Construe the UCC

(a) **The Uniform Commercial Code must be liberally construed and applied to promote its underlying purposes and policies which are:**

(1) **to simplify, clarify, and modernize the law governing commercial transactions;**

(2) **to permit the continued expansion of commercial practices through custom, usage, and agreement of the parties; and**

(3) **to make uniform the law among the various jurisdictions.**

(b) **Unless displaced by the particular provisions of the Uniform Commercial Code, the principles of law and equity, including the law merchant and the law relative to capacity to contract, principal and agent, estoppel, fraud, misrepresentation, duress, coercion, mistake, and bankruptcy.**

Why § 1–103 Matters

§ 1-103 matters first because it makes plain that Article 2 should be liberally interpreted in order to advance the aims of simplifying and clarifying the law governing commercial transactions. No matter that the UCC is sometimes less than clear, it is intended to keep things as simple and straightforward as possible. Hence, as a practice pointer, if your adversary someday puts forth a strained or unduly complicated interpretation of governing Article 2 doctrine, be the voice of reason and remind the court of the § 1-103 imperative to try to keep it simple. Albert Einstein could have been talking about the UCC (he wasn't) when he remarked, *"Everything should be kept as simple as possible. Never simpler than that, but still as simple as possible."*

Second, § 1-103 matters because it clearly provides that unless displaced, the principles of law and equity, such as fraud, duress, detrimental reliance, unjust enrichment, and promissory estoppel continue to apply. In practice, and on an exam, this reminder can be of immeasurable assistance. Sometimes, there will not be an Article 2 provision directly on point to resolve the issue at hand, no matter that the transaction that gave rise to that issue is within Article 2's scope. Alternatively, sometimes the Article 2 provision on point would result in patent unfairness. In those instances, § 1-103 directs you to resolve the matter using supplemental principles of law and equity.

§ 1-201: The UCC Dictionary

In particular, note the following definitions within § 1-201's glossary:

> **Agreement:** § 1-201(3) defines agreement as the bargain of the parties in fact (meaning, what the parties actually bargained for), as determined on the basis of a.) their words, b.) any prior course of performance between them, c.) any prior course of dealing between them and d.) any relevant custom or usage of trade in their industry.

Contract: § 1-201(12) defines the parties' contract as the total legal obligation that results from their agreement. Not all agreements or bargains are enforceable as binding contracts. Only agreements that comport with the requisite Article 2 requirements enjoy the force of law as contracts.

Record: § 1-201(31) defines record as the written or electronic memorialization of the parties' agreement. This definition replaces the earlier Article 2 definition of "writing," which was defined narrowly as "printing, typewriting, or any other intentional reduction to tangible form," and expressly allows for electronic records in contracting.

Hence, use the terms "writing" and "record" interchangeably. When Article 2 calls for a "writing" to authenticate a given transaction, it is referring to authentication in a tangible medium or electronic medium.

Delivery: § 1-201(15) defines delivery as the voluntary transfer of possession. This definition will become important when we take up questions relevant to the parties' performance obligations. To ask, "Did the seller deliver?" is to ask, "Did the seller part with control?"

> **"Delivery" differs from "receipt."** Seller's **delivery** of the goods is to be distinguished from buyer's **receipt** of the goods. A buyer is in receipt of the contracted-for goods only when s/he has taken physical possession of the goods. Thus, it is possible for goods to be delivered (i.e., seller has parted with control) but not yet received. For example, seller places the goods on buyer's doorstep. Seller has delivered. Buyer is not home. Buyer has not yet

received the goods. The difference between delivery and receipt will be important in later chapters examining when the risk of loss of damage or destruction to contracted-for goods passes from seller to buyer.

Good faith: § 1-201(20) imposes a two-prong test for gauging a party's good faith. First, good faith requires honesty in fact. This is a subjective test that asks whether or not the given buyer or seller actually believed that s/he was acting honestly at the particular point in question. Second, the good faith standard requires the "observance of reasonable commercial standards of fair dealing." This is an objective test.

§ 1-303: Meet the Triplets: Course of Performance, Course of Dealing and Trade Usage

(a) A "course of performance" is a sequence of conduct between the parties to a particular transaction that exists if:

(1) the agreement of the parties with respect to the transaction involves repeated occasions for performance by a party; and

(2) the other party, with knowledge of the nature of the performance and opportunity for objection to it, accepts the performance or acquiesces in it without objection.

(b) A "course of dealing" is a sequence of conduct concerning previous transactions between the parties to a particular transaction that is fairly to be regarded as establishing a common basis of understanding for interpreting their expressions and other conduct.

(c) A "usage of trade" is any practice or method of dealing having such regularity of observance in a place, vocation, or trade as to justify an expectation that it will be observed with respect to the transaction in question.

(d) A course of performance or course of dealing between the parties or usage of trade in the vocation or trade in which they are engaged or of which they are or should be aware is relevant in ascertaining the meaning of the parties' agreement, may give particular meaning to specific terms of the agreement, and may supplement or qualify the terms of the agreement. A usage of trade applicable in the place in which part of the performance under the agreement is to occur may be so utilized as to that part of the performance.

(e) Except as otherwise provided in subsection (f), the express terms of an agreement and any applicable course of performance, course of dealing, or usage of trade must be construed whenever reasonable as consistent with each other. If such a construction is unreasonable:

(1) express terms prevail over course of performance, course of dealing, and usage of trade;

(2) course of performance prevails over course of dealing and usage of trade; and

(3) course of dealing prevails over usage of trade.

(f) Subject to § 2-209, a course of performance is relevant to show a waiver or modification of any term inconsistent with the course of performance.

(g) Evidence of a relevant usage of trade of trade offered by one party is not admissible unless that party has

given the other party notice that the court finds sufficient to prevent unfair surprise to the other party.

Why the Triplets Matter: Understanding Course of Performance, Course of Dealing and Trade Usage

A sales contract must not be divorced from its commercial context. Thus, the parties' course of performance, course of dealing and relevant trade usage (in that order) are very important when determining the nature of the bargain struck. For ease of reference in this guide, we refer to those three important predictors of the parties' conduct and expectations as "the triplets."

The Triplets Described

Course of performance is the "sequence of conduct between the parties to a particular transaction that exists if the agreement of the parties with respect to the transaction involves repeated occasions for performance by a party."

How to Find the Parties' Course of Performance

Look for the parties' course of performance whenever the contract calls for repeated occasions for performance. For example, there will be a course of performance between the parties to an installment sales contract, where seller is to deliver in separate units or installments.

For example, Adam enters into a one-year contract that obliges him to deliver a new guitar to Blake on the first of each month. What Blake and Adam do on each of those occasions for performance is relevant to an understanding of what they can reasonably expect with respect to the contract's future occasions for performance. Course of performance is closest to the parties' immediate expectations, and therefore is the most helpful of the triplets.

Course of dealing is the "sequence of conduct concerning previous transactions between the parties to a particular transaction that is fairly to be regarded as establishing a common basis of understanding for interpreting their expressions and other conduct."

How to Find the Parties' Course of Dealing

Course of dealing is found in any prior Article 2 contracts that existed between the buyer and seller that could establish a set of shared expectations or practices to inform this contract.

For example, Adam enters into a contract to sell a guitar to Blake. Last year, in a different contract, Adam sold a drum set to Blake and the year before that in another separate contract Adam sold Blake a clarinet. Those previous sales of instruments establish a course of dealing between Adam and Blake that helps to determine appropriate norms for their behavior on this deal.

Course of dealing looks beyond the four corners of the immediate deal and therefore is more remote in time than any relevant course of performance. Hence, the parties' course of dealing is of lesser significance than any course of performance and of greater significance than trade usage, which more generally applies not just to this buyer and seller but to all those within the given industry or trade.

Trade usage is "any practice or method of dealing having such regularity of observance in a place, vocation or trade as to justify an expectation that it will be observed with respect to the transaction in question."

How to Find Trade Usage

Trade usage is found in the business norms and customs of the industry or trade in question. Trade usage provides a relevant backdrop against which the parties' contract will be interpreted. Still, it is not as close to the parties' expectations as any course of performance they share on this deal or any previous course of dealing that existed between them.

Examples of trade usage might include:

- In the children's clothing industry, sellers know that "delivery June-August" means that 75% of the products are to be delivered by June 1 and the remaining 25% by August 1.
- In the pizza dough trade in New York City, buyers and sellers understand that a 10% discount applies to orders for more than 5,000 units of dough.
- In the plastics industry, contracts typically contain an indemnification clause whereby buyer agrees to indemnify seller for any damages suffered by malfunctions in the equipment.

CHAPTER 3

Five Pillars of Article 2 Construction

We now begin building the Article 2 house of learning. Its foundation rests on five essential pillars. They form the bedrock on which the law of Sales is based. Apply them throughout your review of Article 2 to be sure that your resolution of a given problem within its scope vindicates not only the form but also the spirit of the statute. Moreover, use them to inform your approach to those Article 2 questions that fall between the cracks of the various statutory mandates.

While Karl Llewellyn and his protégés, the UCC's principal architects, did a masterful job of designing Article 2, they could not anticipate every case or controversy. Hence, particularly when in doubt, allow these pillars to inform and become the foundation for your understanding of the law of sales.

Pillar One: Never Divorce the Article 2 Contract from Its Commercial Setting

The UCC's drafters were legal realists, meaning that they aim to codify the law merchant, or the way commercial transactions are actually conducted in the context of the given industry or trade. They did not seek to re-invent the wheel. They sought instead to replicate, in a streamlined and cohesive fashion, the customary norms of commercial exchange. The result that the Code reaches with respect to any particular controversy is not meant to stray from those norms. That's why the triplets (course of performance, course of dealing and trade usage) matter as much as they do in understanding what it is that the parties have agreed to and what it is that they should reasonably expect.

Practice pointer: Since the Code could not anticipate every issue likely to arise in the course of contract formation and performance, sometimes a gap or gray area will come up. Particularly then, always ask, ***How would similarly situated parties have resolved this matter had they explicitly bargained over it?***

Article 2's commitment to legal realism means that the statute endeavors to honor people's reasonable and commonly held expectations. Those expectations are derived from the parties' words (what they promised to do), their actions or conduct (what they actually do), and, when applicable, their prior course of performance, course of dealing and relevant trade usage (the triplets). A contract for the sale of goods should never be divorced from its commercial setting.

Pillar Two: Merchants Are Held to Higher Standards

Article 2 applies to commercial and consumer transactions and to merchants as well as non-merchants. Merchants, who by definition have expertise with respect to the goods in question as well as the norms of commercial exchange, are held to more exacting standards than non-merchants. Why? Because they should know better.

§ 2-104: Defining Who Qualifies as a "Merchant"

> "Merchant" means a person who deals in goods of the kind or otherwise by his or her occupation holds himself or herself out as having knowledge or skill peculiar to the practices or goods involved in the transaction or to whom such knowledge or skill may be attributed by his or her employment of an agent or broker or other intermediary who by his occupation holds himself or herself out as having such knowledge or skill.

The Two Ways to Qualify as a Merchant for Article 2 Purposes

Under § 2-104, one can be labeled a merchant if: (1) he deals in goods that are the subject matter of the given transaction or (2) he holds himself out as having knowledge or skill peculiar to the practices or goods involved in the transaction. Those in the first category include the local shopkeeper, the sales clerk at the department store's watch counter, the cattle trader, and the car dealer. Those in the second category include the plumber who sells a customer a plunger, or the photographer who sells a client a camera. By contrast, a plumber who sells his car is not a merchant for purposes of the car sale and a photographer who sells his sofa is not a merchant for purposes of the sofa sale.

Pillar Three: Unconscionability Doctrine Applies to Abuses During the Formation Stage of an Article 2 Contract

Sometimes a party to an Article 2 contract will argue that he was strong-armed or forced into agreeing to a patently unfair contract or contract provision. Allegations of abuse of bargaining power during the contract's formative process are assessed in accordance with § 2-302's provisions on unconscionability.

For example, suppose that Domino's Pizza's busiest day is Super Bowl Sunday. Knowing that, the week before the Super Bowl, Domino's exclusive cheese supplier tripled the price of its cheese. Domino's has no choice but to agree to the exorbitant price demand. When it later asserts that the agreed-upon price is grossly unfair, Article 2's unconscionability doctrine applies to assess the merits of the claim.

§ 2-302: Unconscionability Doctrine

> **(1) If the court as a matter of law finds the contract or any clause of the contract to have been unconscionable at the time it was made the court may refuse to enforce the contract, or it may enforce the remainder of the contract without the unconscionable clause, or it may so limit the application of any unconscionable clause as to avoid any unconscionable result.**
>
> **(2) When it is claimed or appears to the court that the contract or any clause thereof may be unconscionable the parties shall be afforded a reasonable opportunity to present evidence as to its commercial setting, purpose and effect to aid the court in making its determination.**

Unconscionability Defined

§ 2-302 does not define the term "unconscionable." Hence, to give meaning to the term we turn to the supplemental principles of common law and case law, as § 1-103 would have us do. The case law tells us that unconscionability is rooted in disparity in bargaining power coupled with a contract term or terms that unreasonably favor the party with superior bargaining power.

A term is unconscionable if it is the product of "undue oppression" born of another's disparate bargaining advantage.

Official Comment 1 states that "the basic test is whether, in the light of the general commercial background and the commercial needs of the particular trade or case, the clauses involved are so one-sided as to be unconscionable under the circumstances existing at the time of the making of the contract. The principle is one of the prevention of oppression and unfair surprise."

Never Divorce the Question of What Is Unconscionable from the Contract's Commercial Setting

§ 2-302(2) makes plain that the contract's commercial context is important when determining whether or not a term or terms are unconscionable. Further, it tells us that hindsight is irrelevant. Instead, assess questions of alleged unconscionability based on the facts in existence at the time of the deal's formation. Indeed, the parties must be given the opportunity to brief the question of commercial setting at the time of the making of the contract when asserting or defending against an unconscionability challenge. Since context is everything, when a court refuses to give this opportunity, it has committed reversible error.

Unconscionability Is a Determination of Law, and Therefore Freely Appealable

The freedom to appeal the court's conclusions as to unconscionability is meant to impose a check on a judge's overreaching or abusing its discretion.

If the Court Deems the Contract or Any Clause Contained Therein Unconscionable, It Has Three Options

If a party to the Article 2 contract successfully challenges the contract or any of its clauses as unconscionable or the court, of its own accord, deems the contract infirm for unconscionability, the court has three ways to proceed. It can:

(1) **Nullify the offensive term and enforce the remainder of the contract**

(2) **Limit the application of the offensive clause to avoid any unconscionable result or**

(3) **Void the entire contract**

Example 1: Applying Unconscionability Doctrine

Several months ago, United Airlines ordered 5,000 wool blankets from Travel Ease for United's new routes to Antarctica, which were about to launch. Ordinarily, the blankets sell for $6.00 per unit. When United placed its order, however, a global wool shortage had driven the cost of the blankets up to $20 per unit. Given that its new flights would soon begin operation, United had no choice but to order the blankets for $20 each. Later on, when the wool market leveled out, United argued that the contract's $20 price term is unconscionable. Will it succeed?

No. While unconscionability doctrine would apply to abuses during contract formation, the question of whether or not the price term is unconscionable would depend on the circumstances as they existed at the time of the making of the deal. At that time, market prices were exorbitant. It does not appear that Travel Ease was endeavoring to strong-arm or coerce United into ordering the blankets, nor was it trying to take undue advantage of United's time constraints. Travel Ease is entitled to the benefit of its bargain. Had United not placed its order at that time, presumably Travel Ease could have sold the blankets elsewhere on the open market for approximately the same $20 per unit.

Pillar Four: Abuses During the Performance Stage of an Article 2 Contract Are Regulated by Good Faith Doctrine, Which Is Set Forth in § 1–201(20)

Good faith doctrine applies when unfairness is alleged to have occurred during the deal's performance phase. Now, a given party is not asserting that she was strong-armed into an unfavorable contract, but instead that the other party abused its position when the time for performance came due.

For example, Nutella and its hazelnut provider enter into a contract that calls for November delivery to ensure that Nutella has the hazelnuts in time for its busiest December holiday season. On November 1, its hazelnut seller demands an additional "service charge" for the November delivery. Otherwise, it will not deliver. That alleged abuse is committed during the performance phase of the deal. Thus, it is regulated not by unconscionability doctrine but instead by good faith standards.

§ 1-201(20): The Meaning of Good Faith

> **"Good faith" means honesty in fact and the observance of reasonable commercial standards of fair dealing.**

The Code imposes both a subjective and objective standard for determining a party's good faith. It is subjective insofar as it requires that the given actor actually perform with honesty ("honesty in fact"). But subjective honesty can impose the problem of the "good heart and empty head," meaning that all sorts of inappropriate behavior could satisfy the good faith standard if the actor thought that what he was doing was the right thing to do. Thus, Article 2 adds an objective component to considerations of whether or not a buyer or seller acted in good faith. That actor, in addition to believing that he was doing the right thing, must also have done the right thing as measured by relevant business or commercial standards of fair dealing.

Example 2: Applying Good Faith Standards

Drake orders microphones from Sony, delivery April 1, just in time for the start of Drake's 50 city concert tour. On March 20, Sony tells Drake that it will ship on time only if he agrees to remit an additional hefty surcharge. Will Sony succeed with that demand?

Apply Article 2's good faith standards, and not unconscionability doctrine, to this problem because here the alleged unfairness is taking place during the performance phase of the deal and not at the time of its formation. It seems that Sony is taking unfair advantage of Drake's situation and imminent need for the microphones and thereby acting in defiance of reasonable commercial standards of fair dealing. However, additional facts are needed to learn more about the reasons and circumstances for Sony's insistence on the surcharge. If linked to some independent and unforeseeable contingency that is reasonable under the circumstances, the demand will not be a breach of Sony's duty to perform in good faith.

Pillar Five: The UCC Favors the Practical over the Formalistic

Article 2 is a pragmatic statute. It seeks to honor contracts that concluded with finality. In that pursuit, it discards common law contract doctrines that are unduly rigid or exalt form to the detriment of substance. Thus, for example, Article 2 rejects the common law's "mirror image rule" (which insists that the acceptance of an offer mirror the offer's terms and manner of transmission), the pre-existing duty rule (which requires that post-contract modifications be supported by independent consideration), and other formalistic conceits that can frustrate the parties' intent and reasonable expectations.

CHAPTER 4

Formation of an Article 2 Contract

The Article 2 Formation of Contract Checklist

Use this checklist to determine whether a valid contract for the sale of goods has been properly formed.

- *Has an offer for the purchase or sale of goods been made?* Offer: not defined in Article 2. Use the Restatement (3d) of Contracts definition, contained in § 24 (an offer is a show of willingness to enter into a bargain made in a way that would justify the expectation that acceptance is invited and will close the deal).
- *Has a firm offer been made by a merchant?* Firm offer: § 2-205: applies only to a merchant who promises in a signed writing to keep an offer to buy or sell goods open or firm, typically for a stated period of time, when that promise is unsupported by consideration.

- *Has the offer been properly accepted?* Acceptance: § 2-206: assent may be demonstrated in any manner reasonable under the circumstances, unless the offer clearly indicates precisely how assent must be made.
- *Do the terms of the offer and the terms of the assent conflict?* Battle of the forms: § 2-207. As long as assent is definite and not made conditional on the offeror's agreement to its variant terms, it is a valid acceptance and not a counter-offer. Its variant terms typically drop out unless the deal is between merchants, in which case apply the automatic inclusion rule.
- *Does the agreement have to be in an authenticated record to be enforceable?* Statute of frauds: § 2-201. Applies to contracts for the sale of goods for $500 or more. The writing must indicate that a contract was formed, it must contain a quantity term, and it must be signed by the party against whom enforcement is sought. If an oral deal was struck or the writing is insufficient, see if any of five exceptions to the writing requirement applies (reply doctrine, specially manufactured goods, admission, partial payment, and partial acceptance).
- *Is a party to the contract seeking to contradict or supplement its terms by evidence of some prior or contemporaneous oral or written agreement?* Parol evidence rule: § 2-202. Applies only to final writings, which cannot be contradicted by such evidence but can be explained or supplemented unless so carefully crafted as to be "final,

complete and exclusive." Course of performance, course of dealing, and trade usage are always admissible to explain the writing.

- *Has there been a post-formation change to the contract?* Post-contract modifications: § 2-209. Post-contract changes do not require independent consideration but must be in writing if within the statute of frauds.

The Ingredients of a Valid Article 2 Contract for the Sale of Goods

First, the Offer

Every contract for the sale of goods begins with an offer. Article 2 does not define offer, thereby inviting consultation with supplemental sources (*see* § 1-103 and the accompanying discussion in the preceding chapter). The most often-invoked source is the Restatement (3d) of Contracts, § 24, which defines the offer as "the manifestation of willingness to enter into a bargain, so made as to justify in another the expectation that his or her assent is invited and will conclude the deal."

The Firm Offer: § 2–205

Article 2 defines the firm offer in § 2-205.

§ 2-205: Firm Offer

> An offer by a merchant to buy or sell goods in a signed writing which by its terms gives assurance that it will be held open is not revocable, for lack of consideration, during the time stated or if no time is stated for a reasonable time, but in no event may such period of irrevocability exceed three

months; but any such term of assurance on a form supplied by the offeree must be separately signed by the offeror.

It is important to note that § 2-205 applies only to merchant offerors. Why? Because merchants are held to higher standards and should be held to their promises.

At common law, firm offers unsupported by consideration were unenforceable. Article 2 modifies that harsh result by rendering a merchant's firm offer enforceable no matter that it is unsupported by consideration. A merchant's firm offer rendered in a signed writing but without some consideration remitted in return is enforceable for the time stated or, if no time is stated for a reasonable time, but in no event for longer than three months. By contrast, if that merchant's firm offer rendered in a signed writing is supported by consideration it lasts for the time stated, unconstrained by the three month cap.

Use the Following Three Step Analysis for Assessing a Merchant's Firm Offer

Step one: Is this a merchant offeror? See § 2-104 for the definition of merchant. If so, proceed to step two.

Step two: Has that merchant offeror promised, in a signed record, to keep its offer to buy or sell goods open or firm? If so, proceed to step three.

Step three: Is that firm offer made by the merchant in a signed record supported by independent consideration? If so, it endures for the time stated and if no time is stated it is binding for a reasonable time. If the firm offer is unsupported by consideration, it endures for the time stated and if no time is stated it is binding for a reasonable time, but in no event may the period of irrevocability exceed three months.

Example 1: The Firm Offer

Lily, an artist, offers to sell one of her paintings to Ted for $2,000. Ted is not sure if there is room in his office for the painting. Lily says, "Not a problem. Just let me know when you decide." Ted says, "Would you mind putting that in writing?" Lily obliges the request. The next month Ted tells Lily that he would like the painting. Lily says, "I'm sorry, but I sold it to Barney last week." Can Ted proceed against Lily?

Yes. Apply the three steps contained above. First, Lily, an artist, is a merchant for purposes of selling her paintings. Second, she presumably promised in a signed writing to keep her offer to sell the painting for $2,000 open until Ted decided if he wanted the painting. Third, that firm offer was not supported by independent consideration. Further, it does not indicate the amount of time for which it will endure. A merchant's firm offer made in a signed writing and not supported by consideration endures for a reasonable time if no time is stated but in no event for longer than three months. Here, it would appear that one month is a reasonable period for Lily's firm offer to endure, unless additional facts yet to be learned suggest otherwise.

The Second Ingredient of a Valid Contract for the Sale of Goods: Acceptance

§ 2-206: Offer and Acceptance in Formation of Contract

(1) Unless otherwise unambiguously indicated by the language or circumstances

(a) an offer to make a contract shall be construed as inviting acceptance in any manner and by any medium reasonable in the circumstances;

(b) an order or other offer to buy goods for prompt or current shipment shall be construed as inviting

acceptance either by a prompt promise to ship or by the prompt or current shipping of conforming or non-conforming goods, but such a shipment of non-conforming goods does not constitute an acceptance if the seller seasonably notifies the buyer that the shipment is offered only as an accommodation to the buyer.

The Three Takeaways from § 2–206

(1) Unless the offer clearly indicates otherwise, whether by its express terms or surrounding circumstances, it may be accepted by any reasonable means and manner.

Consistent with the UCC's efforts to replace formalism with pragmatism, § 2-206 rejects the common law's "mirror image" rule. That formulaic rule insisted that a given assent, to succeed in locking in a contract, had to mirror both the offer's terms and its mode of communication. Hence, if the offer was communicated by mail, the assent, to qualify as an acceptance capable of closing the deal, had to be communicated by mail. § 2-206 instead permits acceptance through any means and by any manner appropriate in view of the deal's commercial setting.

(2) The offeror can still be the so-called "master of the offer" by clearly indicating in the offer precisely how acceptance is to be manifested in order to close the deal.

§ 2-206(1) permits the offeror to "unambiguously indicate" how and when acceptance must be communicated to conclude the transaction. But if the offeror does not do that, acceptance is permitted by any means and in any manner reasonable under the circumstances.

(3) Unless it clearly states otherwise, an offer or order to buy goods for immediate or prompt shipment can be accepted in

one of two ways: i.) by prompt promise to ship or ii.) by prompt shipment.

Significantly, in this context even the shipment of nonconforming goods qualifies as an acceptance (and not a counter-offer) and locks in a contract on buyer's terms. Hence, a seller who promptly ships nonconforming goods in response to buyer's order or offer to buy goods for immediate or quick shipment makes and breaches a contract at the same time unless seller makes plain that the shipment is merely an accommodation (in which case it is a counter-offer).

Orders or offers to purchase goods for quick or immediate shipment typically are fraught with a sense of urgency or exigent circumstance. In those instances, at common law an unscrupulous seller could take advantage of the buyer's vulnerability by shipping even substandard or otherwise nonconforming goods without risk. Because of the mirror image rule, that shipment would qualify not as an acceptance but instead as a counter-offer which buyer could take or leave without risk to seller. Thus, a desperate buyer might accept the goods, locking in the contract on seller's terms and thereby relieving seller of liability for breach of contract. Alternatively, buyer could decline to accept, again without legal consequence for seller. § 2-206 endeavors to close the door to the unscrupulous seller. Hence, seller's prompt tender even of nonconforming goods in response to buyer's request for prompt or current shipment qualifies as an acceptance of buyer's offer, thereby locking in a contract and simultaneously breaching that contract, unless seller indicates that the tender is merely an accommodation.

Example 2: Acceptance

A.) Claire texts Saul offering to sell him her used microwave for $300. The next day, Saul calls Claire to say, "That would be great." Has a contract been locked in?

Yes, as long as Saul's assent is reasonable under the circumstances. Without additional facts, there is no reason to believe it to be unreasonable. Remember that § 2-206 discards the mirror image rule, which would have required that to lock in a contract Saul's assent would have to have been communicated by text (mirroring the offer's means of transmission). Thus, Saul's acceptance will close the deal no matter that it is communicated by phone rather than by text.

B.) Quinn emails Bass Pro Shop with the message, "Please ship within twenty-four hours your current stock of Northface UltraThermal sleeping bags." Instead, Bass shipped within twenty-four hours its current stock of soon-to-be discontinued Patagonia sleeping bags. What result?

With its non-conforming shipment, Bass accepted and breached the contract. Quinn made an offer for prompt shipment. By promptly shipping non-conforming goods without any indication that the shipment was tendered merely as an accommodation, Bass accepted and also breached the contract.

What to Do When the Terms of the Offer and Terms of the Acceptance Differ: Apply § 2–207

§ 2-207: Additional Terms in Acceptance or Confirmation

(1) A definite and seasonable expression of acceptance or a written confirmation which is sent within a

reasonable time operates as an acceptance even though it states terms additional to or different from those offered or agreed upon, unless acceptance is expressly made conditional on assent to the additional or different terms.

(2) The additional terms are to be construed as proposals for addition to the contract. Between merchants such terms become part of the contract unless:

(a) the offer expressly limits acceptance to the terms of the offer;

(b) they materially alter it; or

(c) notification of objection to them has already been given or is given within a reasonable time after notice of them is received.

(3) Conduct by both parties which recognizes the existence of a contract is sufficient to establish a contract for sale although the writings of the parties do not otherwise establish a contract. In such case the terms of the particular contract consist of those terms on which the writings of the parties agree, together with any supplementary terms incorporated under any other provisions under this subtitle.

The Context

Sometimes the terms of the offer and the terms of what seems to be an acceptance of the offer do not match up. § 2-207 addresses that problem, commonly referred to as the "battle of the forms" because seller's acknowledgment form contains terms in addition to or different from those contained in buyer's order form (or purchase order).

The Three Questions to Ask When the Terms of the Offer and Terms of the Assent Vary

First, Has a Contract Been Formed No Matter That the Terms of the Seeming Assent Deviate from the Terms Contained in the Offer? To Answer, Apply § 2–207(1).

At common law, because of the mirror image rule, an expression of acceptance that contained variant terms was not an acceptance but instead a counter-offer. Article 2 discards the mirror image rule and instead, in § 2-207(1) provides that an unequivocal and timely expression of acceptance is indeed an acceptance and not a mere counter-offer, no matter that it contains terms additional to or different from those contained in the offer, unless that acceptance is conditioned on assent to its variant terms (in which case it would be deemed a counter-offer).

Second, if the Assent Does Qualify as an Acceptance, Thereby Locking in a Deal, What Becomes of Its Variant Terms? To Answer, Turn to § 2–207(2).

(1) **If one or both parties are non-merchants:** If one or both parties are non-merchants, the variant terms are to be treated as mere proposals for addition to the contract. They will drop out If not explicitly assented to.

(2) **If both parties are merchants:** Recall that merchants are held to higher standards. If the contract is between merchants, § 2-207(2) applies the so-called "automatic inclusion rule," meaning that the variant terms will automatically become part of the contract unless the offer limits assent to the offer's terms, the offeror objects to the variant term(s) within a reasonable time or the variant term(s) materially alters the contract. The exceptions to the rule essentially exclude from automatic exclusion only the most inoffensive and trivial of

variant terms. Do you see why? First, an offer that expressly limits assent to only the offer's terms is exempted from the specter of automatic inclusion. Second, even if the offer did not limit assent only to its terms, all that the offeror need do to preclude automatic inclusion of any variant terms contained in the assent is object to those terms within a reasonable time after notice of them is received. Third, even if the offer did not limit assent only to its terms and the offeror failed to object within a reasonable time to any variant terms contained in the assent, those variant terms will drop out if they materially alter the contract. Official Comment 4 indicates that a term would materially alter the contract if its incorporation without express awareness by the other party would result in surprise or hardship. For example, a clause negating otherwise applicable warranties or limiting remedies or departing from trade usage would work a material alteration.

Third, if the Parties' Writings Do Not Establish a Contract but Their Conduct Does, Turn to § 2–207(3).

Sometimes the term of the offer and the terms of a seeming assent are at an impossible impasse. Merchants have learned to track Article 2's statutory language to include as a matter of standard form boilerplate a clause in the purchase order that states, "This offer expressly limits acceptance to the terms of the offer." Standard form acknowledgments often include a clause that makes acceptance "conditional on assent to its terms." In those situations, apply § 2-207(3). A contract for sale will arise when the parties' conduct recognizes the existence of a contract no matter that their respective forms are at odds. In such instances, the terms of the contract are those on which the writings agree, together with any supplementary terms incorporated by the parties' course of performance, course of dealing, trade usage, or Code gap-fillers (taken up in Chapter Four).

Example 3: The Battle of the Forms

Lucious owns a record company. He sends a purchase order to Bose Sound Equipment for the purchase of sound equipment, purchase price $75,000, delivery March 1. The purchase order contains the statement, "Assent is invited only as to terms contained herein." Bose replies with its standard form acknowledgment, confirming the product, price and delivery date and including a one-time fee of $60 used to enter new customers into Bose's database. The acknowledgment also limits buyer's remedies to repair. Has a valid contract been formed? Why or why not? If so, what are its terms?

Bose accepted with its acknowledgment form, no matter the form's inclusion of variant terms, as long as that form did not state that it was expressly made conditional on buyer's assent to its variant terms. Remember that § 2-207(1) (like § 2-206) rejects the mirror image rule. Hence, an assent can qualify as an acceptance of an offer no matter that it does not mirror precisely the terms of the offer.

Now that we know that a contract has been formed, what becomes of the variant terms contained in the acceptance? § 2-207(2) tells us that when one of the parties is a non-merchant, the variant term(s) drops out. By contrast, between merchants (as here) the variant terms are automatically included unless any one of three exceptions to the automatic inclusion rule applies. Terms that are additional to or different from those contained in the offer will not be included in the contract, even when the contract is between merchants, if the offer expressly limits assent to the offer's terms. Here, Lucious' purchase order did just that. Hence, both variant terms drop out.

Even if the offer had not expressly limited assent to the offer's terms, the limited remedy clause would have dropped out as a material alteration to the contract. Comment 4 to § 2-207 defines a material alteration as a provision whose automatic inclusion would likely result in unfair surprise. More facts would be needed to glean whether the one-time registration fee's inclusion would work a material alteration.

The short answer: a valid contract has been formed for the purchase of the sound equipment, purchase price $75,000 with delivery on March 1, without inclusion of the one-time fee or limitation of remedies clause.

When the Contract for the Sale of Goods Must Be Authenticated by a Record to Be Enforceable: The Statute of Frauds: § 2–201

§ 2-201: Formal Requirements; Statute of Frauds

(1) Except as otherwise provided in this section a contract for the sale of goods for the price of $500 or more is not enforceable by way of action or defense unless there is some writing sufficient to indicate that a contract for sale has been made between the parties and signed by the party against whom enforcement is sought or by his authorized agent or broker. A writing is not insufficient because it omits or incorrectly states a term agreed upon but the contract is not enforceable under this paragraph beyond the quantity of goods shown in such writing.

(2) Between merchants if within a reasonable time a writing in confirmation of the contract and sufficient against the sender is received and the party receiving it has reason to know its contents, it satisfies the requirements of subsection (1) against such party

unless written notice of objection to its contents is given within ten days after it is received.

(3) A contract which does not satisfy the requirements of subsection (1) but which is valid in other respects is enforceable

(a) if the goods are to be specifically manufactured for the buyer and are not suitable for sale to others in the ordinary course of the seller's business and the seller, before notice of repudiation is received and under circumstances which reasonably indicate that the goods are for the buyer, has made either a substantial beginning of their manufacture or commitments for their procurement; or

(b) if the party against whom enforcement is sought admits in his or her pleading, testimony or otherwise in court that a contract for sale was made, but the contract is not enforceable under this provision beyond the quantity of goods admitted; or

(c) with respect to goods for which payment has been made and accepted or which have been received and accepted.

The Context

Unless one of five exceptions applies, a contract for the sale of goods for the price of $500 or more must be authenticated by an appropriate record. The idea behind the statute of frauds is that parties to a bargain tend to realize that when they sign a contract, the deal is binding. Article 2 enforces only those deals intended by the parties to be binding contracts. The writing requirement helps to assure that buyer and seller know what they are getting into when they strike a bargain and signals to the parties that they are concluding a deal "for real."

I am always reminded in this setting of an exchange that my daughter Nina had with the Easter Bunny when Nina was five years old. She had doubts that the Easter Bunny was real, and so she secretly wrote him a letter that said, "Easter Bunny, if you are real, please sign here." Even as a small child, she understood that if he signed on the line provided that he had to be for real. (Thankfully the Easter Bunny did find the note and did sign as requested). Similarly, when parties sign a contract they are committing to its terms. They mean it, for real.

The statute of frauds also exists to protect against people inventing contracts where none existed. Unless the reply doctrine applies, the party to be bound to a contract within the scope of the writing requirement had to have signed an appropriate writing in order to be obliged to honor its terms.

It is important to note that the most recent amendments to the UCC updated and modernized the writing requirement to ensure its continued relevance in a digital age. Hence, the term "writing" includes electronic communications such as e-mails and PDFs. Electronic "writings," digital communications and writings are now referred to as "records."

The Purpose of the Statute of Frauds

The purpose of the writing requirement is to prevent the fabrication of contracts where none existed. By contrast, the statute of frauds is not intended to bar the enforcement of contracts actually formed, albeit without a sufficient writing. That is important. What that means is that the writing requirement must not be used as a formalistic barrier to a contract's enforceability. If the parties did conclude with finality an oral contract for the sale of goods, or reduced their contract to a writing that fails to meet the requirements of § 2-201, their contract nonetheless should be binding. If one of the parties to a contract that is not authenticated by an appropriate writing tries disingenuously to plead the statute of frauds as a defense to the contract's enforcement, the five exceptions to the writing requirement jump in to help to render the deal binding.

The Three Step Approach to Use When Applying the Statute of Frauds

Step One: Is This a Contract for the Sale of Goods for $500 or More?

If so, go to § 2-201 and proceed to step two.

Step Two: Is There a Sufficient Writing or Writings to Authenticate the Contract?

Specifically, the writing or composite of writings must indicate that a contract for the sale of goods was made between the parties, it must contain a quantity term and it must be signed by the party against whom enforcement is sought (the defendant), The Code drafters deemed quantity the term must susceptible to fabrication or fraud. Hence, to qualify as a valid writing, the contract must reference quantity. Other terms, including price, can be supplied by the parties' course of performance, course of dealing or trade usage or the Code's gap-filler provisions. If the writing or writings do not meet the three invariable requirements of § 2-201(1), go to step 3.

Step Three: Do One of the Following Five Exceptions to the Writing Requirement Set Forth in § 2–201(2) and (3) Apply?

(1) **The first exception to the statute of frauds: the reply doctrine (§ 2-201(2)).** Prior to Article 2, the only type of writing to satisfy the statute of frauds was one signed by the party against whom enforcement was sought. Thus, a party who wrote a letter of confirmation of a given deal would be bound but the recipient of that confirmation, who never signed, would not be bound. An unscrupulous recipient of such a confirmatory memo could simply wait for the time of performance to come due to decide whether to perform or not, knowing that the deal was enforceable only against sender. The Code's reply doctrine changes that inequitable result and deems a letter of confirmation or confirmatory memo a reliable method of satisfying the statute of frauds.

To invoke the reply doctrine successfully, four requirements must be met:

a.) the contract must be between merchants (another example of how merchants are held to higher standards)

b.) a letter of confirmation or confirmatory memo must be sent within a reasonable time and the party receiving it must have reason to know of its contents

c.) the confirmation must meet the three requirements for a binding writing so that it would be sufficient to bind its sender (meaning that the writing must contain a quantity term, it must evidence a contract for the sale of goods and it must be signed by its sender) and

d.) the party receiving the confirmation must not object to its contents in writing within ten days after it is received.

Example 4: The Reply Doctrine

Walter, a chemist, places a telephone order with Total Labs for the purchase of two dozen Bunsen burners at a total cost of $2,000. Walter emails a quick note to Total Labs that states, "Thank you for taking my order for two dozen Bunsen burners, cost $2,000, delivery at your earliest convenience." The goods never arrive. When Walter phones Total Labs to ask about the order, it replies, "We didn't acknowledge anything in writing and don't have any stock left." Is Total Labs liable for breach of contract?

Yes. Whenever a party to an alleged Article 2 contract seeks to deny a deal's enforcement on the basis that there is no appropriate writing to authenticate it, apply the statute of frauds analysis set forth earlier. First, do we need a writing to enforce this alleged deal? Yes. This is an alleged contract for the sale of goods for $500 or more. Do we have an appropriate writing that evidences a contract for the sale of goods, contains a quantity term and is signed by the party against whom enforcement is sought? No. Total Labs never signed any writing to authenticate this deal. Third, do any of the five exceptions to the statute of frauds apply? Yes. The reply doctrine applies to bind Total Labs. Run through the reply doctrine's three steps. First, this is a deal between merchants. Walter, a chemist, is a merchant for purposes of goods related to his profession, skill and training. Second, there is a memo in confirmation of the deal that would be capable of binding its sender, Walter. His email contains a quantity term, evinces a contract for the sale of goods and is deemed signed by Walter if sufficiently electronically marked. The UCC defines "signed" to include electronic markings. Third, the recipient, Total Labs, did not object in writing to that memo's contents within three days of its receipt. Walter's confirmation binds Walter and Total Labs.

(2) **The second exception to the statute of frauds: admissions (§ 2-201(3)(b)).** The party against whom enforcement is sought

cannot admit the fact of the contract in court pleadings and simultaneously claim the benefit of the statute of frauds. Recall that the purpose of the statute of frauds is to prevent fraud, not serve as a formalistic impediment to the enforcement of a contract actually formed (albeit orally). Hence, one who admits in pleadings, testimony or otherwise in court that a contract was made is bound by that admission, up to the quantity of goods admitted.

(3) **The third exception to the statute of frauds: specially manufactured goods (§ 2-201(3)(a)).** Contracts for the sale of specially manufactured goods are exempted from the writing requirement if four criteria are met: a.) the goods were specially manufactured for the buyer, b.) they are not suitable for sale to others, c.) the circumstances reasonably indicate that the goods are for the buyer and d.) before repudiation the seller has made a substantial beginning in their manufacture.

(4) **The fourth exception to the statute of frauds: partial payment (§ 2-201(3)(c).** Absent a writing, an otherwise valid contract is enforceable to the extent to which payment has been made and accepted.

(5) **The fifth exception to the statute of frauds: partial delivery (§ 2-201(3)(c)).** Absent a writing, an otherwise valid contract is enforceable with respect to goods which have been received and accepted.

The Parol Evidence Rule: When a Party Tries to Contradict or Supplement a Final Contract's Terms: § 2–202

§ 2-202: Final Written Expression: Parol or Extrinsic Evidence

Terms with respect to which the confirmatory memoranda of the parties agree or which are otherwise set forth in a

writing intended by the parties as a final expression of their agreement with respect to such terms as are included therein may not be contradicted by evidence of any prior agreement or of a contemporaneous oral agreement but may be explained or supplemented

> **(1) by course of performance, course of dealing, or usage of trade (§ 1-303); and**
>
> **(2) by evidence of consistent additional terms unless the court finds the writing to have been intended also as a complete and exclusive statement of the terms of the agreement.**

The parol evidence rule is intended to give certainty to written agreements entered into with care and formality and to protect against perjury. It provides that terms set forth in a final writing (also known as a partially integrated writing) cannot be contradicted at trial by evidence of any alleged prior agreement or contemporaneous oral agreement but can be supplemented by evidence of consistent additional terms unless the court deems the final writing so meticulously well-crafted as to be "a complete and exclusive statement of the terms of the agreement." Such "final, complete and exclusive" contracts (also referred to as fully integrated) cannot be supplemented by evidence of consistent additional terms. However, all final writings, whether partially or fully integrated, can be explained or supplemented by relevant course of performance, course of dealing or trade usage.

The Three Takeaways from § 2–202

(1) Evidence extrinsic to a final writing will be excluded from evidence if it contradicts the terms of a final writing and is contained in a prior agreement or contemporaneous oral agreement.

(2) A final writing that is deemed by the court to be only partially integrated may be supplemented by evidence of consistent additional terms but a final writing that is deemed by the court to be fully integrated ("final, complete and exclusive") cannot be supplemented by such evidence.

(3) Unless carefully negated in the contract, course of performance, course of dealing and trade usage are freely admissible to explain or supplement both partially integrated and fully integrated writings.

Telling the Difference Between Partially Integrated and Fully Integrated Contracts

The parol evidence rule can become confounding first because it makes a distinction between "final writings"—meaning partially integrated contracts—and contracts that are final but also so meticulously well-crafted as to be deemed by the court as "intended also as a complete and exclusive statement of the terms of the agreement"—meaning fully integrated. To tell the difference between partially and fully integrated contracts, courts use a multi-factored approach.

Factors to Consider to Determine the Extent of the Writing's Integration

Relevant factors include:

(1) whether both parties were represented by counsel

(2) the sophistication of the transaction

(3) the price of the goods

(4) the amount of time available to comport the writing to negotiations

(5) and the presence or absence of a merger or integration clause. A merger or integration clause is a provision in the contract that recites that it is the parties' "final, complete and exclusive understanding." Because merger clauses are usually boilerplate, their presence alone is not dispositive.

Why the Extent of the Contract's Integration Matters

Partially integrated contracts can be supplemented by evidence of alleged prior or contemporaneous consistent additional terms. Fully integrated writings cannot be explained or supplemented by evidence of consistent additional terms.

Still . . .

All final contracts, whether partially or fully integrated, can be explained or supplemented by evidence relevant to course of performance, course of dealing and trade usage (the triplets) unless that evidence has been carefully negated or displaced in the contract.

Thus, to Assess Admissibility Under the Parol Evidence Rule the Court Engages in Two Tasks

First the court categorizes the parties' contract. Is it a final writing and, if so, is that final writing partially or fully integrated? Second, the court categorizes the given proffer (meaning what it is that a party to the contract seeks to introduce into evidence to either explain or contradict its terms.) If that proffer contradicts the final contract's terms it is inadmissible. By contrast, if the proffer is supplemental or explanatory it is admissible unless the court has determined that the contract is fully integrated. Remember too that if the proffer is relevant to the triplets the court will rule it admissible to explain even a fully integrated contract unless the proffer has been carefully negated or displaced in the contract.

Example 5: Applying the Parol Evidence Rule

Negan negotiates with Ezekiel to purchase equipment. During negotiations Ezekiel indicated that he should be able to deliver within 24 hours of Negan placing his order. On May 1, the parties enter into a contract for the equipment. The contract contains a merger clause and the delivery date is recited as May 10. When the equipment fails to arrive on May 2, Negan sues for breach of contract and at trial seeks to introduce evidence of the parties' conversation during negotiations wherein Ezekial indicated that delivery should occur within 24 hours of Negan's placement of his order. What result?

This problem requires analysis of the parol evidence rule. Negan is seeking to revoke the promise that Ezekiel made during the contract's negotiation. When a party to a final contract endeavors to contradict or supplement that final contract by evidence of some understanding that was allegedly arrived at before or around the same time as the contract was concluded, go to § 2-202.

Apply the two steps for parol evidence analysis:

First, classify the writing. Unless there are additional facts to suggest otherwise, this contract is presumably final and partially integrated. The presence of the merger clause is not dispositive, but helps to establish that the writing is at least partially integrated.

Second, categorize what it is that Negan is seeking to introduce into the contract. He is seeking to introduce evidence that the delivery date was May 2 and not May 10, on the basis of the conversation that he had with Ezekiel during negotiations. That proffer contradicts the contract's delivery date of May 10. A final contract cannot be contradicted by evidence of an agreement allegedly reached by the parties prior to the actual finalization of the contract. The idea here is that if the parties had truly understood that delivery would be accomplished by May 2, that understanding would have been reflected in their final contract. It was not. Hence, the presumption is that the earlier delivery date term was ultimately discarded by the parties and superseded by the May 10 date. Otherwise, if final contracts could be contradicted by anything and everything that transpired in the lead up to the deal's closing, few parties would have incentive to actually close deals with precision and care.

Post-Contract Modifications: § 2–209

§ 2-209: Modification, Rescission and Waiver

(1) An agreement modifying a contract within this Article needs no consideration to be binding.

(2) A signed agreement which excludes modification or rescission except by a signed writing cannot be otherwise modified or rescinded, but except as between merchants such a requirement on a form supplied by the merchant must be separately signed by the other party.

(3) The requirements of the statute of frauds section of this Article (§ 2-201) must be satisfied if the contract as modified is within its provisions.

(4) Although an attempt at modification or rescission does not satisfy the requirements of subsection (2) or (3) it can operate as a waiver.

(5) A party who has made a waiver affecting an executory portion of the contract may retract the waiver by reasonable notification received by the other party

that strict performance will be required of any term waived, unless the retraction would be unjust in view of a material change of position in reliance on the waiver.

The Context

Sometimes the parties will change or modify their contract **after** the deal is finalized. When you are presented with a change in terms alleged to have occurred **after** the contract was struck, turn to § 2-209. By contrast, when the alleged change in terms is said to have occurred in the negotiation phase before or as the final deal was being struck apply the parol evidence rule of § 2-202.

Three Important Takeaways on Post-Contract Modifications

(1) **You do not need independent consideration to render a post-contract change binding.** Consistent with Article 2's attempt to discard undue formalism, consideration is not needed for a post-contract modification to be enforceable. § 2-209(1) represents a departure from the common law of contract's pre-existing duty rule, which required that post-contract changes be supported by independent consideration to be binding.

(2) **Post-contract modifications must be in writing to be enforceable when the contract says so or the contract as modified is for $500 or more.** While post-contract modifications need not be supported by consideration, they do have to be in writing in two circumstances: 1.) if the original contract requires that all modifications be in writing or 2.) if the contract, as modified, is within the statute of frauds. § 2-209 incorporates the statute of frauds (§ 2-201) into its terms. Hence, if the contract, as modified, is for the sale of goods for

$500 or more, the change must be evidenced in a valid writing. If the alleged modification is not contained in a valid writing, check to see if one of the exceptions to the statute of frauds applies. Run through the reply doctrine, specially manufactured goods, admissions, partial payment and partial acceptance exceptions to see if any one of those is available on your facts to take the modification out of the writing requirement.

(3) **Post-contract modifications must be made in good faith.** The Official Comments to § 2-209 emphasize that all post-contract modifications must meet the test of good faith imposed by Article 2. Comment 2 to § 2-209 provides that the use of bad faith to evade contract performance is prohibited, "and the extortion of a 'modification' without legitimate commercial reason is ineffective as a violation of the duty of good faith." § 1-201(20) in turn defines good faith to mean "honesty in fact and the observance of reasonable commercial standards of fair dealing." That is both a subjective and objective determination.

Example 6: Post-Contract Modifications

Negan contracted with Ezekiel to purchase various food products, total cost $2,000. The contract provided that delivery would be accomplished by May 2. On May 1, Ezekiel met with Negan to ask if delivery on May 10 would be ok. Negan said, "Sure." The next day, when the goods did not arrive, Negan cancelled the contract, alleging breach by Ezekiel. What result?

§ 2-209 applies when there is an alleged post-contract change in the contract's terms. While the change in the term for delivery does not need to be supported by consideration, it does have to comport with the statute of frauds because the contract, even with the alleged modification, is for $500 or more. It is not in writing. Still, the admissions exception to the writing requirement could apply here if matters become litigious and Negan is asked under oath about the change in delivery date. If he answers truthfully, that admission displaces the need for a writing.

CHAPTER 5

The Content of the Article 2 Contract

Once a contract for the sale of goods has been formed, questions can arise with respect to its terms. For example, sometimes the terms are ambiguous or missing. Article 2 helps to resolve questions pertaining to the contract's content in the § 2-300s.

The Approach to Use to Discern the Article 2 Contract's Terms

- ***Express terms control.*** The contract's express provisions are binding unless found to be unconscionable (*see* § 2-302) or in violation of applicable law (*see* § 1-103).
- ***If terms are missing, apply this three-step approach:***

  (1) Did the parties intend to contract with finality no matter the absence of certain term(s)? If so, proceed to step 2.

(2) Go to the triplets (relevant course of performance, course of dealing and trade usage) to supply the missing term(s) (*see* § 1-303 and § 2-208).

(3) If the triplets are unavailing, go to the Article 2 gap-fillers, contained in the § 2-300s.

- ***Article 2's gap-fillers: Article 2 supplies the following terms when there is a gap in the contract that cannot be filled by the triplets:***

  (1) When price is unspecified: § 2-305

  (2) When time for delivery is unspecified: § 2-309

  (3) When place for delivery is unspecified: § 2-308

  (4) When manner of delivery is left open: § 2-307

  (5) When other specifications as to delivery are left open: § 2-311

  (6) When time and place for payment are left open: § 2-310

  (7) When quantity is left to be defined by seller's output or buyer's requirements: § 2-306

  (8) When an unforeseen event renders performance impossible or impracticable: § 2-508, §§ 2-613—616 (*see* chapter six)

  (9) When the quality of the goods is undefined: Article 2's warranty provisions: §§ 2-312—318 (*see* chapter seven)

Working with Article 2's Gap-Fillers

Sometimes, whether by design or inadvertence, the parties to an Article 2 contract leave terms unspecified or absent. In those instances, before resorting to Article 2's gap-fillers be sure to ascertain first whether the parties intended to close the deal, no matter the absence of a term or terms. You will be able to glean that intent on the basis of the document itself as well as the parties' words and conduct. If it is clear that the parties intended to contract with finality, determine next whether their course of performance, course of dealing or applicable trade usage (the triplets) can supply the missing term or terms. (*See* chapter two for a detailed discussion of the triplets.) If the triplets are unavailing, turn to Article 2's gap-fillers. Each of those is discussed below.

When Price Is Unspecified: § 2–305

§ 2-305: Open Price Term

(1) The parties if they so intend can conclude a contract for sale even though the price is not settled. In such a case the price is a reasonable price at the time for delivery if:

(a) nothing is said as to price; or

(b) the price is left to be agreed by the parties and they fail to agree; or

(c) the price to be fixed in terms of some agreed market or other standard as set or recorded by a third person or agency and it is not so set or recorded.

Sometimes the price for the goods contracted for is left open. Recall that the statute of frauds (§ 2-201) requires only that contracts within its scope contain some reference to quantity. All other terms including price can be supplied, assuming of course that the parties intended to close the deal no matter the absence of a precise price term.

Note that § 2-305 provides that the price to be supplied is not necessarily the market price at the time and place of delivery but instead a reasonable price at that time. Most courts add "and place" to § 2-305's provision that "the price is a reasonable price at the time [and place] for delivery."

When Time for Delivery Is Unspecified: § 2–309

§ 2-309: Absence of Specific Time Provisions; Notice of Termination

(1) The time for shipment or delivery or any other action under a contract if not provided in this Article or agreed upon shall be a reasonable time.

(2) Where the contract provides for successive performances but is indefinite in duration it is valid for a reasonable time but unless otherwise agreed may be terminated at any time by either party.

(3) Termination of a contract by one party except on the happening of an agreed event requires that reasonable notification be received by the other party and an agreement dispensing with notification is invalid if its operation would be unconscionable.

This Code gap-filler indicates that the time for shipment or delivery is a reasonable time. It also provides that an open-ended contract that calls for repeated performances may be terminated by either party upon giving reasonable notice. Termination differs from cancellation. Termination means that the contract has been amicably ended for reasons other than breach. By contrast, cancellation is a remedy that is exercised in response to a breach.

When Place for Delivery Is Left Open: § 2–308

§ 2-308: Absence of Specified Place for Delivery

Unless otherwise agreed

(a) the place for delivery of goods is the seller's place of business or if he or she has none his residence; but

(b) in a contract for sale of identified goods which to the knowledge of the parties at the time of contracting are in some other place, that place is the place for the delivery; and

(c) documents of title may be delivered through customary banking channels.

In the absence of agreement, delivery is to occur at seller's place of business, unless the contract is for the sale of identified goods located in some other place. When that is the case, the place for delivery is the place where the goods are located. Goods are identified to the contract when they are distinguishable from the world of comparable goods.

For example, if the contract calls for the sale of grapes grown on a designated two-acre vineyard in northern California, the grapes are identified to the contract. If the contract does not stipulate the place for delivery and the triplets are unavailing, the place for delivery is that vineyard where the goods are located.

When the Manner of Delivery Is Unspecified: § 2–307

§ 2-307: Delivery in Single Lots or Several Lots

Unless otherwise agreed all goods called for by a contract for sale must be tendered in a single delivery and payment is due only on such tender but where the circumstances give either party the right to make or demand delivery in lots the price if it can be apportioned may be demanded for each lot.

The presumption here is that the contracted-for goods are to be tendered in a single delivery with payment due on tender. However, the UCC does acknowledge that sometimes the circumstances rightly give either party the right to make or demand delivery in separate lots, as when the quantity of goods to be tendered is exceedingly large.

When the Time for Payment Is Unspecified: § 2–310

§ 2-310: Open Time for Payment

Unless otherwise agreed

(a) payment is due at the time and place at which the buyer is to receive the goods; and

(b) if the seller is authorized to send the goods he or she may ship them under reservation, and may tender the documents of title, but the buyer may inspect the goods after their arrival before payment is due unless such inspection is inconsistent with the terms of the contract (§ 2-513); and

(c) if delivery is authorized and made by way of documents of title otherwise than by subsection (b) then payment is due regardless of where the goods are to be received (i) at the time and place at which the buyer is to receive delivery of the tangible documents or (ii) at the time the buyer is to receive delivery of the electronic documents and at the seller's place of business or if none, the seller's residence; and

(d) where the seller is required or authorized to ship the goods on credit the credit period runs from the time of shipment but post-dating the invoice or delaying its dispatch will correspondingly delay the starting of the credit period.

When the contract fails to stipulate the time for payment, buyer must pay at the time and place that he takes possession of the goods.

When Quantity Is Determined by Buyer's Requirements or Seller's Output: § 2–306

§ 2-306: Output, Requirements and Exclusive Dealings

(1) A term which measures the quantity by the output of the seller or the requirements of the buyer means such actual output or requirements as may occur in good faith, except that no quantity unreasonably disproportionate to any stated estimate or in the absence of a stated estimate to any normal or otherwise comparable prior output or requirements may be tendered or demanded.

(2) A lawful agreement by either the seller or the buyer for exclusive dealing in the kind of goods concerned imposes unless otherwise agreed an obligation by the seller to use best efforts to supply the goods and by the buyer to use best efforts to promote their sale.

While contracts for the sale of goods within the scope of the statute of frauds must contain some reference to quantity, it is permissible for the parties to specify that quantity is to be determined on the basis of seller's output (an output contract) or buyer's requirements (a requirements contract). § 2-306 governs output and requirements contracts.

The Output Contract Defined

In an output contract, quantity is determined on the basis of seller's output or production. For example, buyer promises to purchase half of the peanut butter that seller makes on a weekly basis, or buyer agrees to buy 15% of seller's annual soybean crop. You will know that it is an output contract when quantity is determined on the basis of the answer to the question *what will the giver deliver?* In an output contract buyer says, *"Seller, if you make it I'll take it."*

The Requirements Contract Defined

In a requirements contract, quantity is determined on the basis of buyer's needs. For example, seller, a brick maker, promises to supply buyer, a builder, with buyer's quarterly needs for bricks. You will know that it is a requirements contract when quantity is determined on the basis of the answer to the question *what do you require buyer?*

The Potential for Abuse in a Requirements or Output Contract

Sometimes a seller in an output contract or buyer in a requirements contract will take advantage of a market shift and manipulate its respective output or requirements. Abuse can arise when a seller's output or buyer's requirements are not actual. For example, to take advantage of a market shift in its favor, buyer in a requirements contract precipitously increases its requirements so that it can stockpile the goods. Alternatively, now that the market has shifted in seller's favor, seller in an output contract suddenly speeds up its production to yield exceedingly high output. In other cases, seller might suddenly cease production or buyer might claim to no longer have a need for the goods. Thus, abuse can also be found in the presence of a wholesale withdrawal by either buyer or seller.

How § 2–306 Protects Against Abuse

To protect against abuse or manipulation, all output and requirements must be actual and must be made in good faith. In addition, even if actual and rendered in good faith, any output or requirement must not be unreasonably disproportionate to any stated estimate or otherwise standard or comparable prior output or requirements.

Exclusive Dealing Output or Requirements Contracts

Sometimes a § 2-306 output or requirements contract will be an exclusive dealing contract. For example, an exclusive dealing requirements contract would oblige buyer to purchase only from seller all of buyer's needs for a particular good. An exclusive dealing output contract would oblige seller to sells its entire output of a designated good only to buyer.

Built into every exclusive dealing output or requirements contract is an element of vulnerability. Hence, § 2-306(2) provides that unless otherwise agreed every exclusive dealing output and requirements contract oblige the parties to do even more than perform in good faith. Each must use best efforts and be particularly diligent. In an exclusive dealing arrangement seller impliedly promises to use best efforts to supply the goods and buyer implicitly promises to use best efforts to promote their sale.

Best efforts means more than acting in good faith. It requires that all reasonable means be exhausted in order to properly perform the contract. What is or is not tantamount to best efforts is a fact-specific determination and depends on the total mix of circumstances to surround the given transaction.

CHAPTER 6

The Gap-Fillers That Excuse Seller from the Contract

The Context

Sometimes an unforeseen event renders seller's performance of an Article 2 contract impossible or, while not impossible, impracticable. In those instances, there usually won't be a provision in the parties' contract to indicate how best to proceed. That is because the event or circumstance that has now arisen to render seller's performance so difficult was never anticipated when the contract was formed. The UCC fills that gap in the parties' contract with its provisions on excuse doctrine. Here, we are asking when seller will be excused from its contracted-for duties because of the occurrence of an unforeseen event or contingency.

How to Apply Excuse Doctrine

Use the following Article 2 sections to answer questions relevant to when seller will be excused from the contract without liability because of some intervening event or circumstance that renders its performance either impossible or so difficult as to be impracticable.

- ***Impossibility of performance:*** § 2-613 applies when goods identified to the contract have suffered casualty through no fault of either party and before the risk of that loss passed to buyer. It applies to relieve seller of its contractual obligations when its performance has been rendered impossible through no fault of its own.
- ***Risk of loss:*** § 2-509 contains the rules relevant to the question of when the risk of the goods' damage or devastation passes from seller to buyer. If the risk of loss had already passed to buyer when the goods suffered casualty, buyer must pay for them and hopefully has insurance to indemnify it for its losses.
- ***Impracticability of performance:*** § 2-615 applies when seller's performance has been rendered exceedingly difficult or impracticable because of the occurrence of some event not foreshadowed in the parties' bargaining process, such as a labor strike, embargo or governmental moratorium. Here, seller's performance is not impossible, strictly speaking, but because of the occurrence of that unforeseeable contingency it has become very, very challenging.
- ***Failure of means of payment or method of delivery:*** § 2-614 applies when a matter secondary to the heart of the contract, such as the means of payment or method of delivery for the goods, is no longer available. In such cases, seller's performance typically is not excused and a commercially equivalent substitute means of payment or method of delivery must be tendered and accepted.

Impossibility of Performance: § 2–613

§ 2-613: Casualty to Identified Goods

> Where the contract requires for its performance goods identified when the contract is made, and the goods suffer casualty without fault of either party before the risk of loss passes to the buyer then
>
> (a) if the loss is total the contract is avoided; and
>
> (b) if the loss is partial or the goods have so deteriorated as no longer to conform to the contract the buyer may nevertheless demand inspection and at his or her option either treat the contract as avoided or accept the goods with due allowance from the contract price for the deterioration or the deficiency in quantity but without further right against the seller.

The Context

§ 2-613 applies when the goods identified to the contract suffer damage or devastation through no fault of either party and before the risk of that loss has passed to the buyer. For example, seller contracts with buyer for the sale of the Chagall painting *The Promenade*. Shortly thereafter, a fire breaks out at the warehouse where the painting is stored, destroying it. If the risk of that loss has not yet passed to buyer and the painting was destroyed through no fault of seller, § 2-613 will apply to excuse seller from its performance obligation and free it without liability from the terms of the contract. In other words, buyer won't be able to successfully sue seller for its nonperformance of the contract. When seller is excused from performance, the contract is discharged.

A Three-Step Technique to Apply When Contracted-For Goods Suffer Casualty

Step One: Are the Goods Contracted for "Identified" to the Contract?

A good is identified when it is distinguishable from the world of similarly situated goods. In the example above, the painting is identified to the contract. It is only that painting, and no other painting, that will satisfy the contract's terms.

Example 1: Identifying Identified Goods

Wolfgang Puck contracts with Restaurant Supplies Co. for the purchase of 20 dozen standard dinner plates. When the time for delivery arrives Restaurant Supplies Co. contacts Wolfgang to inform him that the plates that they had in mind to satisfy the contract had been shattered when the shelf they were on collapsed. Are the plates identified to the contract? No. The contract required the tender of standard dinner plates. Presumably those are fungible goods. Hence, seller is obliged to find a substitute source to satisfy the contract.

Example 2: Identifying Identified Goods

Wolfgang Puck contracts with Francois Truffles, a specialty grower of rare mushrooms grown on two designated acres in southern California, for the purchase of its fall harvest of mushrooms. Are the mushrooms identified to the contract? Yes. If that acreage suffers a drought, for example, so that the harvest is not available, seller should be excused from its performance obligation.

Step Two: If the Contracted-For Goods Are Identified to the Contract, Have They Suffered Damage or Devastation Through No Fault of Either Party?

Official Comment 1 to § 2-613 defines fault to include negligence in addition to willful wrongdoing. Fault is liberally defined to encourage the parties to the contract to exercise reasonable care with respect to the goods contracted for. If the identified goods have suffered casualty as a proximate cause of seller's carelessness, seller will not be excused and will be liable for breach of contract.

Example 3: Finding Fault

Suppose in example 2, above, that the harvest suffered a drought because seller neglected to turn the irrigation system on. Seller will not be excused and will instead be liable for breach of contract, no matter that the identified goods are no longer available. A contrary rule could encourage sellers to be "remiss" by design, perhaps as a way out of what has proven to be a less than desirable deal.

Step Three: Has the Casualty to the Identified Goods Occurred Before the Risk of That Loss Passed to the Buyer?

If the risk of loss had already passed from seller to buyer at the time that the goods are destroyed or damaged, excuse doctrine does not apply and buyer must remit payment for the goods (no matter that they are compromised or no longer exist). In those instances, the presumption is that the buyer insured the goods and that insurance will cover the loss. By contrast, if the risk of loss had not yet passed from seller to buyer at the time of the casualty to identified goods, excuse doctrine does apply to relieve seller of his performance obligation.

§ 2–509 Applies to Answer the Question of When the Risk of Loss Passes from Seller to Buyer

§ 2-509: Risk of Loss in the Absence of Breach

(1) Where the contract requires or authorizes the seller to ship the goods by carrier

(a) if it does not require him to deliver them at a particular destination, the risk of loss passes to the buyer when the goods are duly delivered to the carrier even though the shipment is under reservation (§ 2-505); but

(b) if it does require him or her to deliver them at a particular destination and the goods are there duly tendered while in the possession of the carrier, the risk of loss passes to the buyer when the goods are there duly so tendered as to enable the buyer to take delivery.

(2) Where the goods are held by a bailee to be delivered without being moved, the risk of loss passes to the buyer

(a) on the buyer's receipt of possession or control of a negotiable document of title covering the goods; or

(b) on acknowledgment by the bailee of the buyer's right to possession of the goods; or

(c) after his receipt of possession or control of a non-negotiable document of title or other direction to deliver in a record, as provided in subsection (4)(b) of § 2-503.

(3) In any case not within subsection (1) or (2), the risk of loss passes to the buyer on his or her receipt of the

goods if the seller is a merchant; otherwise the risk passes to the buyer on tender of delivery.

§ 2–509 Provides Four Answers to the Question "When Does the Risk of Loss Pass from Seller to Buyer?"

(1) In a shipment contract, the risk of loss passes once seller places conforming goods into the hands of the carrier. § 2-509(1)(a).

A shipment contract arises whenever the contract requires shipment of the goods without the added specification that seller assure the goods' arrival at a particular destination. In commercial exchanges the term "F.O.B. (free on board) seller's place of business" is a shorthand reference to the fact that this is a shipment contract.

For example, Penny, a pharmaceutical representative in Pasadena, California, contracts with Hackensack Medical Center, a hospital in Hackensack, New Jersey, promising to ship 400 Epi-Pens, FOB California. That shorthand reference indicates that this is a shipment contract. California is seller's place of business. The risk of any loss to the goods passes from seller to buyer once the conforming goods leave seller's place of business and are placed with the carrier. That could occur when, for example, UPS or FedEx picks up the shipment from Penny's office. If the goods suffer damage thereafter, that is buyer's problem and buyer's loss. Buyer will likely have insurance to indemnify it for any losses, or be able to proceed directly against the carrier if fault or negligence can be attributed to it. Still, buyer is obliged to remit payment for the goods to seller, no matter their damaged or devastated condition.

(2) ***In a destination contract, the risk of loss does not pass from seller to buyer until the conforming goods arrive at their specified destination, so tendered as to enable buyer to take delivery. § 2-509(1)(b).***

A destination contract arises whenever the contract specifies that seller assure the goods' arrival at a particular destination. In commercial exchanges the term "F.O.B. (free on board) buyer's place of business" is a shorthand reference to the fact that this is a destination contract.

For example, Penny, a pharmaceutical representative in Pasadena, California, contracts with Hackensack Medical Center, a hospital in Hackensack, New Jersey, promising to ship 400 Epi-Pens, FOB New Jersey. That shorthand reference indicates that this is a destination contract. New Jersey is buyer's place of business. The risk of any loss to the goods passes from seller to buyer only when the conforming goods arrive at their destination so that buyer can take delivery. If the goods suffer damage while in transit, seller remains responsible for tendering conforming Epi-Pens to buyer. It might be able to plead impossibility of performance, and thereby be relieved of its performance obligation, but only if the Epi-Pens were identified to the contract, meaning that they are distinguishable from any other alternative source of supply for Epi-Pens. Otherwise, the presumption is that Penny should be able to procure an alternative source of supply to satisfy this contract. She thus remains liable to buyer.

(3) ***If the goods are in a warehouse or other storage facility and are to be delivered without being moved, the risk of loss passes from seller to buyer on buyer's receipt of a document of title covering the goods. § 2-509(2).***

For example, Penny contracts to sell Hackensack Medical Center 400 Epi-Pens, delivery at Warehouse 4 in Perth Amboy,

NJ. The risk of loss passes from Penny to Hackensack once it is in physical possession of the documents necessary to authorize it to pick up the goods. If the goods suffer thereafter through no fault of seller, that is buyer's loss to absorb. It remains obliged to remit payment.

(4) ***In all other instances, the risk of loss passes from seller to buyer on buyer's receipt of the goods if seller is a merchant or, if seller is a non-merchant, on seller's tender of delivery, no matter that buyer is not yet in receipt of the goods. § 2-509(3).***

This catch-all provision applies when, for example, the goods are to be picked up at seller's place of business.

For example, Penny contracts to sell Hackensack Medical Center 400 Epi-pens. The contract provides that Hackensack is to send its agent to Penny's corporate headquarters to pick up the goods. Because seller is a merchant, the risk of loss to the goods passes when buyer takes physical possession of the goods. Thus, if Penny phones buyer and says, "The goods are here. Come by anytime this week to pick them up," but the goods suffer damage or destruction before buyer arrives to collect them, the risk of that loss resided with seller. It will be excused from its performance obligation only if it was without fault and the product is identified to the contract. Otherwise, it will be liable for breach of contract if it fails to perform.

Impracticability of Performance: § 2–615

§ 2-615: Excuse by Failure of Presupposed Conditions

Except so far as a seller may have assumed a greater obligation and subject to the preceding section on substituted performance:

(a) Delay in delivery or non-delivery in whole or in part by a seller who complies with paragraphs (b) and (c) is not a breach of his duty under a contract for sale if performance as agreed has been made impracticable by the occurrence of a contingency the non-occurrence of which was a basic assumption on which the contract was made or by compliance in good faith with any applicable foreign or domestic governmental regulation or order whether or not it later proves to be invalid.

(b) Where the causes mentioned in paragraph (a) affect only a part of the seller's capacity to perform, he or she must allocate production and deliveries among his or her customers but may at his option include regular customers not then under contract as well as his own requirements for further manufacture. He or she may so allocate in any manner which is fair and reasonable.

(c) The seller must notify the buyer seasonably that there will be delay or non-delivery and, when allocation is required under paragraph (b), of the estimated quota thus made available for the buyer.

The Context

§ 2-615 applies when seller's performance, while not impossible, is rendered exceedingly difficult or commercially impracticable because of the occurrence of some unforeseeable event. That event, to form the basis for excusable non-performance, must not have been foreshadowed in the bargaining process. The greater the inference that the problem complained of was predictable, the lesser the inference that impracticability doctrine will apply to relieve seller from its performance obligation. The idea here is that when the given event was foreseeable during the contract's formation, seller is presumed to have assumed the risk of its occurring, promising to perform notwithstanding its occurrence.

Official Comment 4 to § 2-615 provides that "increased cost alone does not excuse performance unless the rise in cost is due to some unforeseen contingency which alters the essential nature of the performance." Similarly, a market shift will not excuse performance unless attributable to some unforeseeable event such as a governmental moratorium or embargo.

Example 4: Impracticability Doctrine

Sheldon, an astrophysicist employed by Cal Tech places an order on behalf of the astrophysics department with Celestron for the purchase of a Starcrest Telescope. Shortly thereafter, a workers' strike erupts at Celestron's main factory that renders it very difficult for it to complete Sheldon's order. Does excuse apply to relieve Celestron of its performance obligation?

It depends. First, if the labor unrest was foreshadowed in the parties' bargaining process the presumption is that seller promised to perform no matter the occurrence of the strike. Hence, it would not be relieved of liability for breach of contract if it failed to perform. By contrast, if the strike was a "contingency the non-occurrence of which is a basic assumption on which the contract was formed," meaning that it was not foreseeable, seller may be able to plead impracticability if it can show that it would not be able to provide an alternative without immense hardship. That inquiry is fact-specific.

When the Means of Delivery or Payment Fails: § 2–614

§ 2-614: Substituted Performance

(1) Where without fault of either party the agreed berthing, loading, or unloading facilities fail or an agreed type of carrier becomes unavailable or the agreed manner of delivery otherwise becomes commercially impracticable but a commercially reasonable substitute is available, such substitute performance must be tendered and accepted.

(2) If the agreed means or manner of payment fails because of domestic or foreign governmental regulation, the seller may withhold or stop delivery unless the buyer provides a means or manner of payment which is commercially a substantial equivalent. If delivery has already been taken, payment by the means or in the manner provided by the regulation discharges the buyer's obligation unless the regulation is discriminatory, oppressive or predatory.

The Context

Sometimes the means of delivery or manner of payment specified in the parties' contract is no longer available when the time for delivery or payment comes due. In those instances, § 2-614 seeks to preserve the essence of the deal notwithstanding that unanticipated failure. That is because delivery and payment methods are considered tangential matters that should not affect the heart of the contract.

The Code provides that if the contractually-specified manner of delivery is no longer available but a commercially reasonable substitute method of delivery is available, performance will not be excused and the substitute mode of delivery must be tendered and accepted. If the agreed upon means of payment is no longer available because of governmental regulation, seller is within its rights to withhold or stop delivery until buyer provides a commercially equivalent way to pay.

CHAPTER 7

The Gap-Fillers to Determine the Goods' Quality

The Context

Here we consider the Code's warranty provisions. Those apply to help to determine the quality of the goods contracted-for. We assess the warranty provisions as gap-fillers because in a number of instances they can apply by implication and thus be imputed to a seller of goods no matter the absence of an explicit representation as to the goods' quality in the parties' contract.

The Warranties' Checklist

- ***The warranty of title:*** § 2-312 provides that a seller warrants that she has good and rightful title to the goods, meaning that she is the owner (and not merely a possessor) of the goods that she now purports to sell.
- ***Express warranties:*** § 2-313 provides that a seller is bound by her statements or promises of fact (as opposed to opinion) that help to form the basis for the parties' bargain.

- ***The implied warranty of merchantability:*** § 2-314 provides that a merchant seller implicitly promises that the goods contracted-for are merchantable, meaning that they would pass without objection in the industry or trade in which those goods are routinely dealt.
- ***The implied warranty of fitness for a particular purpose:*** § 2-315 provides that a seller who knows or should know of buyer's particular purpose for the goods and that buyer is relying on seller to select suitable goods implicitly promises that the goods are suitable for buyer's particular needs.
- ***Construe warranties cumulatively:*** § 2-317 indicates that more than one warranty can apply to the given circumstances and that warranties are to be construed as cumulative and whenever possible as consistent with each other.
- ***Disclaimers of warranties:*** § 2-316 indicates the ways that a promise regarding the goods' quality might be disclaimed or modified.
- ***The limitation of privity:*** § 2-318 applies to assess whether the given warranty applies when the user of the goods contracted-for is not the buyer but the buyer's family member, guest, employee or invitee.

The Warranty of Title: § 2–312

§ 2-312: Warranty of Title and Against Infringement

(1) Subject to subsection (2) there is in a contract for sale a warranty by the seller that

(a) the title conveyed shall be good, and its transfer rightful; and

(b) the goods shall be delivered free from any security interest or other lien or encumbrance of which the buyer at the time of contracting has no knowledge.

(2) A warranty under subsection (1) will be excluded or modified only by specific language or by circumstances which give the buyer reason to know that the person selling does not claim title in himself or that he is purporting to sell only such right or title as he or a third person may have.

The Context

Every seller of goods warrants or promises that he owns the goods contracted-for and has the power to sell those goods. In other words, the seller of goods promises that the title he is conveying to the buyer is good, free of any outstanding liens or claims that could be asserted by others. § 2-312 applies in tandem with Article 9 of the UCC, which pertains whenever a creditor has a security interest or lien in debtor's goods to collateralize or back up the creditor's extension of value to that debtor.

Example 1: The Warranty of Title

Jon Snow, a knight, orders chest armor from Byzantine Supplies. The goods arrive but later that day a creditor shows up at Jon's door, stating, "We lent money to Byzantine Supplies. It gave us as collateral a lien in its chest armor supplies. It has failed to repay us. We are here to collect the goods that you received this morning." What result?

If Jon has to surrender the goods to the creditor, he has a claim against Byzantine Supplies for breach of the warranty of title. Byzantine implicitly promised in its contract with Jon that it had good and clear title or ownership to the goods. It did not. The armor is the subject of the creditor's lien, of which Byzantine presumably has knowledge.

Express Warranties: § 2–313

§ 2-313: Express Warranties by Affirmation, Promise, Description, Sample

(1) Express warranties by the seller are created as follows:

(a) Any affirmation of fact or promise made by the seller to the buyer which relates to the goods and becomes part of the basis of the bargain creates an express warranty that the goods shall conform to the affirmation or promise.

(b) Any description of the goods which is made part of the basis of the bargain creates an express warranty that the goods shall conform to the description.

(c) Any sample or model which is made part of the basis of the bargain creates an express warranty that the whole of the goods shall conform to the sample or model.

(2) It is not necessary to the creation of an express warranty that the seller use formal words such as "warrant" or "guarantee" or that he have a specific intention to make a warranty, but an affirmation merely of the value of the goods or a statement purporting to be merely the seller's opinion or commendation of the goods does not create a warranty.

An Overview

A seller of goods can create an express warranty in any one of three ways: i.) by what she says about the goods, whether orally or in writing; ii.) by providing a description of the goods through for example a brochure, pictures or charts of technical specifications or iii.) by providing a sample or model of the goods. A sample is actually drawn from the bulk of the goods themselves while a model is presented as a replica of the goods.

Four Important Points to Know About Express Warranties

(1) ***Seller's statements of fact can be express warranties. Seller's mere opinions cannot.*** To qualify as an express warranty, seller's representation about the goods must be more than mere opinion or puffery. It must be a statement of fact that becomes part of the basis of the bargain. As Official Comment 3 points out, it is presumed that seller's affirmations of fact about the goods are part of the bargain that is struck. It is not necessary that seller have had the intent to create an express warranty, nor is it necessary that buyer prove actual reliance.

For example, Byzantine Supplies' salesperson tells Jon Snow, who just tried on chest armor for possible purchase, *"That chest plate is virile and exudes confidence in its wearer."* That statement is mere puffery or opinion. It is not actionable. Article 2 presumes that a reasonable buyer would understand that those words ought to be taken with a healthy dose of skepticism. By contrast, when Byzantine Supplies tells Jon Snow, "This chest plate is made of titanium steel. It is rust-proof." Those statements of fact qualify as express warranties. Article 2 presumes that promises of that nature are apt to be part of the reason that buyer makes this purchase. When the chest plate turns out to rust easily because it is made of silver, Jon Snow has a claim for breach of express warranty.

(2) ***Consistent with Article 2's aim to honor substance over form, creation of an express warranty does not depend on seller's using magic words such as "I promise" or "We warrant" or "I guarantee."***

(3) ***Any statements of fact that seller makes to buyer after the deal is struck do not qualify as express warranties.*** (Remember that an express warranty, to be such, must be part of the basis of the bargain that is struck.) Instead, post-contract promises about the goods' quality are analyzed as post-contract modifications within the scope of § 2-209, discussed in chapter three.

(4) ***§ 2-313 will often coincide with § 2-202, the parol evidence rule (discussed in chapter three).*** For example, seller might make various statements relevant to the goods' quality during the negotiation phase of the deal and then seek to disavow those statements once the deal is struck. In those instances, the parol evidence rule can become relevant to determine when and whether those statements would be admissible to establish the quality of the goods contracted for.

For example, as Jon Snow was thinking about whether to make the purchase of the chest plate, seller says, *"If you don't like it once you take it home, you have thirty days no questions asked to return it for a full refund."* Thereafter Jon Snow enters into a contract for the purchase of the chest plate. He decides after it is delivered that he really does not like it as much as he thought. When he returns it, Byzantine Supplies indicates that it will issue a refund only for cause. They add that Jon Snow's mere change of heart is not good cause. When Jon Snow reminds seller of the promise it made about the no questions asked refund, seller replies, *"That's not in the contract.*" In the subsequent lawsuit, Jon Snow will seek to introduce evidence of the conversation that he and seller had prior to finalizing the contract. Its admissibility turns on the degree of the contract's integration. Presumably this contract is partially integrated, and therefore capable of supplementation by evidence of seller's promise as a consistent additional term.

The Implied Warranty of Merchantability: § 2–314

§ 2-314: Implied Warranty: Merchantability; Usage of Trade

(1) Unless excluded or modified (§ 2-316), a warranty that the goods shall be merchantable is implied in a contract for their sale if the seller is a merchant with respect to goods of that kind. Under this section the serving for value of food or drink to be consumed either on the premises or elsewhere is a sale.

(2) Goods to be merchantable must be at least such as

(a) pass without objection in the trade under the contract description; and

(b) in the case of fungible goods, are of fair average quality within the description; and

(c) are fit for the ordinary purposes for which such goods are used; and

(d) run, within the variations permitted by the agreement, of even kind, quality and quantity within each unit and among all units involved; and

(e) are adequately contained, packaged, and labeled as the agreement may require; and

(f) **conform to the promise or affirmations of fact made on the container or label if any.**

(3) **Unless excluded or modified (§ 2-316) other implied warranties may arise from course of dealing or usage of trade.**

The Context

A merchant seller implicitly promises that the goods she is selling are merchantable, meaning suitable for their ordinary purposes. The Official Comments to § 2-314 indicate that goods sold by a merchant "in a given line of trade must be of a quality comparable to that generally acceptable in that line of trade." Official Comment 2. Hence, the meaning of merchantability depends on custom, industry practice and trade usage. The parties' relevant course of performance and course of dealing can also set standards of merchantability. Moreover, price is a relevant gauge of the quality of the goods contracted for, insofar as most buyers expect to get what they pay for. Official Comment 7.

The Implied Warranty of Merchantability Applies to the Sale of Food and Drink

§ 2-314 applies to food products consumed in restaurants as well as purchased from a merchant's inventory. Previously, liability would attach only when the problem complained of was caused by a foreign substance such as, for example, the presence of a nail in a bowl of chili. Liability would not attach when the harm complained of was caused by a natural by-product such as, for example, a cow bone fragment in a hamburger. Today, most courts will impose liability irrespective of whether the offending particle was foreign or natural if a similarly situated reasonable user would not reasonably have anticipated the substance's presence.

For § 2–314 to Apply, Four Elements Must Be Met

(1) This must be a contract for the sale of goods, and not for services.

(2) Seller must be a merchant as that term is defined in § 2-104.

(3) That merchant seller implicitly promises that the goods contracted for are suitable for their customary or usual purposes.

(4) The warranty must not have been modified or otherwise disclaimed pursuant to § 2-316, discussed *infra.*

The Implied Warranty of Fitness for a Particular Purpose: § 2–315

§ 2-315: Implied Warranty: Fitness for Particular Purpose

> **Where the seller at the time of contracting has reason to know any particular purpose for which the goods are required and that the buyer is relying on the seller's skill or judgment to select or furnish suitable goods, there is unless excluded or modified under the next section an implied warranty that the goods shall be fit for such purpose.**

The Context

Remember that the implied warranty of merchantability has a merchant seller implicitly promising that the goods sold are fit for their ordinary purposes. For example, a sweater is suitable for its ordinary purposes when it can be worn without incident. A sweater that when worn would cause an ordinary buyer to develop skin lesions is not merchantable. The implied warranty of fitness for a particular purpose, by contrast, has the seller implicitly promising that the goods are suitable for this buyer's particular needs. For example, when seller knows that buyer needs a sweater able to provide UV sun protection and buyer relies on seller to find just the right sweater for that purpose, seller has betrayed the implied warranty of fitness for a particular purpose when the sweater proves inadequate for that need.

The implied warranty of fitness for a particular purpose will apply when: (1) seller knows or has reason to know of the particular purpose that buyer has in mind for the goods and (2) buyer actually relies on seller's expertise to select suitable goods. This is the only warranty that depends for its successful assertion on buyer's demonstrating reliance in fact on seller's judgment. Hence, the greater the buyer's reliance on its own independent research and judgment the lesser the inference that buyer actually relied on seller's expertise to make the purchase.

Official Comment 1 states that the question of whether or not this warranty arises in a given case is one of fact to be determined by an assessment of the circumstances surrounding the contract's formation. The relevant consideration becomes whether "the circumstances are such that the seller has reason to realize the purpose intended or that the reliance exists." Official Comment 1. The buyer, in turn, must actually be relying on the seller.

Notice that § 2-315 is not limited to merchant sellers. As Official Comment 4 points out, "Although normally the warranty will arise only where the seller is a merchant with the appropriate 'skill or judgment,' it can arise as to non-merchants where this is justified by the particular circumstances."

Warranties Are to Be Construed Cumulatively: § 2–317

§ 2-317: Cumulation and Conflict of Warranties Express or Implied

> Warranties whether express or implied shall be construed as consistent with each other and as cumulative, but if such construction is unreasonable the intention of the parties shall determine which warranty is dominant. In ascertaining that intention the following rules apply:
>
> (a) Exact or technical specifications displace an inconsistent sample or model or general language of description.
>
> (b) A sample from an existing bulk displaces inconsistent general language of description.
>
> (c) Express warranties displace inconsistent implied warranties other than an implied warranty of fitness for a particular purpose.

The Context

Often, more than one warranty will apply to a given set of facts. § 2-317 provides that to the extent possible warranties should be interpreted as cumulative and as consistent with each other.

Example 2: Construing Warranties Cumulatively

Jon Snow purchases chest armor from Byzantine Supplies. He tells seller that the chest armor must be able to withstand extreme heat at temperatures as high as 160 degrees Fahrenheit. Seller helps Jon Snow to select suitable chest armor, telling him, "*This product will withstand temperatures as high as 180 degrees Fahrenheit.*" Jon Snow purchases the chest plate and wears it into battle only to discover that it melts even at temperatures of 80 degrees Fahrenheit. Advise Jon Snow.

Jon Snow should be able to proceed for breach of several warranties. Warranties are to be construed cumulatively, pursuant to § 2-317. Seller made and breached an express warranty under § 2-313 when it promised that the product could withstand temperatures as high as 180 degrees Fahrenheit. That is an affirmation of fact that formed part of the basis of the bargain. It proved to be untrue. Seller, a merchant, implicitly promised that the chest armor would be suitable for its ordinary purposes. Those ordinary purposes presumably include battle in ordinary temperatures. The product proved unfit for that purpose. Seller breached the implied warranty of fitness for a particular purpose under § 2-315 since it knew of buyer's particular needs and that buyer was relying on its judgment when selecting goods suitable to meet those needs. The goods were not fit for buyer's particular purposes.

Disclaiming Warranties: § 2–316

§ 2-316: Exclusion or Modification of Warranties

(1) **Words or conduct relevant to the creation of an express warranty and words or conduct tending to negate or limit warranty shall be construed wherever reasonable as consistent with each other; but subject to the provisions of this Article on parol or extrinsic evidence (§ 2-202) negation or limitation is inoperative to the extent that such construction is unreasonable.**

(2) **Subject to subsection (3), to exclude or modify the implied warranty of merchantability or any part of it the language must mention merchantability and in case of a writing must be conspicuous, and to exclude or**

modify any implied warranty of fitness the exclusion must be by a writing and conspicuous. Language to exclude all implied warranties of fitness is sufficient if it states, for example, that, "There are no warranties which extend beyond the description on the face hereof."

(3) Notwithstanding subsection (2)

(a) unless the circumstances indicate otherwise, all implied warranties are excluded by expressions like "as is," "with all faults" or other language which in common understanding calls the buyer's attention to the exclusion of warranties and makes plain that there is no implied warranty; and

(b) when the buyer before entering into the contract has examined the goods or the sample or model as fully as he or she desired or has refused to examine the goods there is no implied warranty with regard to defects which an examination ought in the circumstances to have revealed to him or her; and

(c) an implied warranty can also be excluded or modified by course of dealing or course of performance or usage of trade.

(4) Remedies for breach of warranty can be limited in accordance with the provisions of this Article on liquidation or limitation of damages and on contractual modification of remedy (§ 2-718 and § 2-719).

The Context

Often, the seller of goods will attempt to negate or displace any warranties that might otherwise apply. It is possible for a seller to sometimes effectively disclaim warranties by its words and/or actions.

How and When a Warranty Can Be Effectively Disclaimed

The implied warranty of merchantability can be disclaimed orally or in writing, but the language of disclaimer must mention the word "merchantability" and the disclaimer, if in writing, must be conspicuous. A disclaimer of the implied warranty of fitness for a particular purpose need not use specific language but the disclaimer must be in a conspicuous writing.

Implied warranties can also be excluded when the goods in question are described as *"irregular"*, *"as is"*, *"with all faults"* or by other language or circumstances that commonly would be understood as signaling to the buyer that no implied warranties exist. For example, buyer goes to a used car lot and sees a car that has a sign on its windshield indicating, "AS IS." That sort of language, taken in context, should alert buyer to the fact that there might well be risks associated with the purchase and that buyer should take care to carefully inspect the car.

§ 2-316 makes plain that when the language of disclaimer and the language of express warranty conflict, the express warranty controls. For example, suppose that the contract states that buyer has agreed to purchase a dryer. The contract also recites that "seller hereby disclaims all warranties." When a washer arrives instead, seller has breached the contract and cannot rely on the warranty disclaimer to justify its nonconforming tender.

The Limitation of Privity: § 2–318

§ 2-318: Third Party Beneficiaries of Warranties Express or Implied

Alternative A

> A seller's warranty whether express or implied extends to any natural person who is in the family or household of his buyer or who is a guest in his home if it is reasonable to expect that such person may use, consume or be affected by the goods and who is injured in person by breach of the warranty. A seller may not exclude or limit the operation of this section.

Alternative B

> A seller's warranty whether express or implied extends to any natural person who may reasonably be expected to use, consume or be affected by the goods and who is injured in person by breach of the warranty. A seller may not exclude or limit the operation of this section.

Alternative C

> A seller's warranty whether express or implied extends to any person who may reasonably be expected to use, consume or be affected by the goods and who is injured by breach of the warranty. A seller may not exclude or limit the operation of this section with respect to injury to the person of an individual to whom the warranty extends.

The Context

Sometimes someone other than the buyer of the goods will suffer harm when the goods are not as warranted. For example, it may be that the buyer's child, employee or houseguest is injured when the goods fail to comport with the specifications promised.

Questions of so-called "horizontal privity" arise in those instances and are governed by § 2-318. By contrast, questions of vertical privity arise when a buyer or remote user seeks to proceed against the allegedly defective product's manufacturer or distributor. Article 2 is silent with respect to questions of vertical privity, leaving those to supplemental sources of law such as tort law and more specifically products liability law.

§ 2–318's Three Alternatives

§ 2-318 gives states three options to choose from. Alternative A takes the narrowest approach to questions of horizontal privity and extends warranty protection to personal injuries sustained by members of buyer's family, household and household guests. Alternative B extends warranty protection for personal injuries to a broader group, including persons who might reasonably be expected to come into contact with the goods. For example, buyer's landscaper, injured by a defective garden hose, would be protected under Alternative B but not Alternative A. Alternative C, the most generous of the alternatives presented, extends warranty protection to the same group as Alternative B but includes protection for economic as well as personal injury.

CHAPTER 8

Performance of an Article 2 Contract for the Sale of Goods

The Context

The parties' performance obligations are contained in the 2-500s and 2-600s of the statute. Stated most succinctly, seller performs by getting the right goods to the right place at the right time. Buyer performs by accepting the conforming goods and paying for them. Often, however, something goes wrong on the road to performance of the contract. In that case, several Article 2 sections intersect to provide a framework for analysis.

A Checklist of the Issues Related to Performance of the Article 2 Contract

Set forth below are the UCC sections to apply when assessing the parties' performance obligations:

- **Begin with § 2-503**, which imposes upon seller the duty to tender conforming goods in a timely manner.

- Once seller has tendered delivery, **turn to § 2-513 and § 2-512**, which apply to buyer's right to inspect the goods tendered. Buyer will know whether seller's tender is conforming by inspecting the goods in accordance with § 2-512 and 2-513.
- **If seller tendered conforming goods on time, buyer is obliged to accept those goods (acceptance in this context is defined in § 2-606)** and pay for them, in accordance with § 2-607.
- If seller failed to tender conforming goods on time, **buyer's options depend on whether or not buyer accepted those goods.** Apply § 2-606 to determine whether, by his words or conduct, buyer can be deemed to have accepted the goods.
- If seller tendered nonconforming goods and buyer has accepted those goods under § 2-606, **apply § 2-607 to assess the consequences of acceptance**. A buyer who has accepted: i.) must remit payment for the goods (no matter their nonconformity), ii.) loses the right to reject the goods under § 2-601 and instead can try to revoke the acceptance under § 2-608, iii.) must notify seller of the goods' nonconformity or be barred from any remedy and iv.) bears the burden of proving that the goods were nonconforming at the time of tender.
- **If seller tendered nonconforming goods and buyer has accepted those goods under § 2-606, buyer cannot reject the goods under § 2-601 but can try to revoke his acceptance under § 2-608.**
- **If seller tendered nonconforming goods and buyer has not accepted those goods under § 2-606, buyer**

can reject the goods by complying with § 2-601 to § 2-605.

- Finally, a seller who tenders nonconforming goods and now faces buyer's rejection or revocation of those goods will sometimes have the opportunity to cure or correct the defect(s) complained of. **Apply the standard for cure set forth in § 2-508 to determine if seller in such cases can be given that second chance to get the right goods to buyer.**

Seller's Performance Obligations: To Get the Right Goods to the Right Place at the Right Time: § 2–503

§ 2-503: Manner of Seller's Tender of Delivery

(1) Tender of delivery requires that the seller put and hold conforming goods at the buyer's disposition and give the buyer any notification reasonably necessary to enable him or her to take delivery. The manner, time and place for tender are determined by the agreement and this Article, and in particular

(a) tender must be at a reasonable hour, and if it is of goods they must be kept available for the period reasonably necessary to enable the buyer to take possession; but

(b) unless otherwise agreed the buyer must furnish facilities reasonably suited to the receipt of the goods.

(2) Where the case is within the next section respecting shipment tender requires that the seller comply with its provisions.

(3) Where the seller is required to deliver at a particular destination tender requires that he or she comply with subsection (1) and also in any appropriate case tender documents as described in subsection (4) and (5) of this section.

(4) Where goods are in the possession of a bailee and are to be delivered without being moved

(a) tender requires that the seller either tender a negotiable document of title covering such goods or procure acknowledgment by the bailee of the buyer's right to possession of the goods; but

(b) tender of the buyer of a non-negotiable document of title or of a record directing the bailee to deliver is sufficient tender unless the buyer seasonably objects, and except as otherwise provided in Article 9 receipt by the bailee of notification of the buyer's rights fixes those rights as against the bailee and all third persons; but risk of loss of the goods and of any failure by the bailee to honor the non-negotiable document of title or to obey the direction remains on the seller until the buyer has had a reasonable time to present the document or direction, and a refusal by the bailee to honor the document or to obey the direction defeats the tender.

(5) Where the contract requires the seller to deliver documents

(a) he or she must tender all such documents in correct form, except as provided in this Article with respect to bills of lading in a set (subsection (2) of § 2-323); and

(b) tender through customary banking channels is sufficient and dishonor of a draft accompanying or associated with the documents constitutes non-acceptance or rejection.

§ 2–503's Essential Takeaway

The most important takeaway from § 2-503 is that seller performs by making conforming goods reasonably available to buyer. The goods tendered must conform with respect to both quality and quantity. Seller makes goods reasonably available when seller notifies buyer of their availability and holds them for a reasonable period of time to allow buyer to retrieve them or ships them pursuant to buyer's instructions.

Determining Whether Seller Tendered Conforming Goods: Buyer's Right to Inspect Under § 2–512 and § 2–513

§ 2-512: Payment by Buyer Before Inspection

(1) Where the contract requires payment before inspection non-conformity of the goods does not excuse the buyer from so making payment unless

(a) the non-conformity appears without inspection; or

(b) despite tender of the required documents the circumstances would justify injunction against honor under the provisions of this subtitle (§ 5-109(b)).

(2) Payment pursuant to subsection (1) does not constitute an acceptance of goods or impair the buyer's right to inspect or any of his or her remedies.

§ 2-513: Buyer's Right to Inspection of Goods

(1) Unless otherwise agreed and subject to subsection (3), where goods are tendered or delivered or identified to the contract for sale, the buyer has a right before payment or acceptance to inspect them at any reasonable place and time and in any reasonable manner. When the seller is required or authorized to send the goods to the buyer, the inspection may be after their arrival.

(2) Expenses of inspection must be borne by the buyer but may be recovered from the seller if the goods do not conform and are rejected.

(3) Unless otherwise agreed the buyer is not entitled to inspect the goods before payment when the contract provides

(a) for delivery "C.O.D." or on other like terms; or

(b) for payment against documents of title, except where such payment is due only after the goods are to become available for inspection.

(4) A place or method of inspection fixed by the parties is presumed to be exclusive but unless otherwise expressly agreed it does not postpone identification or shift the place for delivery or for passing the risk of loss. If compliance becomes impossible, inspection shall be as provided in this section unless the place or method fixed was clearly intended as an indispensable condition failure of which avoids the contract.

The Intersection of § 2–512 and § 2–513

§ 2-513 provides that unless otherwise agreed in the contract or prescribed by the circumstances, buyer has the right to inspect seller's tender before having to remit payment for the goods. A "C.O.D." or "cash on delivery" transaction is one of those circumstances where buyer must pay for the goods on delivery, even before inspecting them, unless the goods' defect is in plain view and detectable on sight. § 2-512 provides that in "C.O.D." transactions, buyer's payment for the goods does not qualify as acceptance of those goods.

By analogy, a buyer who purchases goods online typically remits payment at the time of purchase, before the goods arrive for inspection. Whether buyer is obliged to pay on delivery or pay in advance, buyer's payment alone does not mean that buyer has accepted the goods. Whether he chooses to exercise the opportunity or not, buyer must be afforded a reasonable chance to inspect the goods tendered before buyer can be found to have accepted those goods. Acceptance and the consequences of acceptance are contained in § 2-606 and § 2-607 and discussed later in this chapter. Buyer cannot be deemed to have accepted and suffer the rather significant consequences of acceptance until buyer has had a meaningful chance to examine the goods.

Four Points to Know About Buyer's Right to Inspect the Goods Contracted-For

The four most important takeaways from § 2-513 are:

(1) Unless the contract states otherwise, buyer bears the cost of inspection. If the goods turn out to be nonconforming, buyer can recover those costs as incidental damages under § 2-715.

(2) The parties are free to stipulate in their contract the designated time, place and manner of inspection.

(3) In the absence of a contract provision on point, buyer is within its rights to inspect at any reasonable

place and time and in any reasonable manner. What is or is not reasonable depends on the circumstances and on the parties' course of performance, course of dealing and industry custom (the triplets).

(4) Inspection is not mandatory, but a buyer who declines the opportunity to inspect the goods tendered or who fails to inspect in a timely manner will suffer the consequences of having accepted the goods, no matter their nonconformity, and may be precluded from a remedy. The consequences of acceptance are set forth in § 2-607, discussed later in this chapter.

Example 1: Buyer's Right to Inspect

Marnie purchases a guitar C.O.D. for her upcoming concert tour. The guitar is delivered, Marnie remits payment to the courier and stores the guitar in its delivery box in her closet. Several weeks later, now that the tour is about to begin, she unpacks the guitar and sees that it is missing a string. Advise Marnie on her rights.

Marnie's payment on delivery of the guitar was required pursuant to the contract's C.O.D. term under § 2-512. Payment is not acceptance. Buyer has a right to inspect before accepting the goods under § 2-606. However, § 2-513 states that inspection must take place at a reasonable time, and presumably at the time of tender or shortly thereafter. Here, Marnie waited several weeks before even opening the package. That delay is likely to be deemed unreasonable in view of the circumstances. Hence, Marnie may have accepted the goods under § 2-606 by signaling by her actions that the tender was suitable. More on the consequences of acceptance later in this chapter.

When Seller Has Tendered Conforming Goods, Buyer Must Accept and Pay for Them: § 2–606

§ 2-606: What Constitutes Acceptance of Goods

(1) Acceptance of goods occurs when the buyer

(a) after a reasonable opportunity to inspect the goods signifies to the seller that the goods are conforming or that he or she will take or retain them in spite of their non-conformity; or

(b) fails to make an effective rejection (subsection (1) of § 2-602), but such acceptance does not occur until the buyer has had a reasonable opportunity to inspect them; or

(c) does any act inconsistent with the seller's ownership; but if such act is wrongful as against the seller it is an acceptance only if ratified by him or her.

(2) Acceptance of a part of any commercial unit is acceptance of that entire unit.

The Meaning of Acceptance in the Performance Setting

Acceptance under § 2-606, in the context of assessing the parties' performance obligations, is very different from acceptance as that term is defined in the formation phase of the contract under § 2-206. § 2-206, discussed earlier, applies to determine how assent of an offer can be manifested in order to close the deal. By contrast, § 2-606 is relevant to the determination of whether a buyer to a sales contract has actually accepted seller's tender of the goods that are the subject of the transaction. Acceptance here means that buyer exercises dominion and control over the goods (by for example storing, using or cleaning them) or does any other act inconsistent with seller's ownership (such as displaying the tendered goods in a shop window or lending them to another).

When buyer's inspection reveals that the goods are conforming, § 2-606 obliges buyer to accept and pay for those goods. Moreover, buyer can be deemed to have accepted even when the goods tendered are non-conforming. In those instances, buyer may have accepted by words, conduct or simply by default, by failing to properly reject non-conforming goods as prescribed by § 2-601 to 2-605, covered later in this chapter.

Putting Together § 2–606, § 2–512 and § 2–513: A Methodical Approach in Eight Steps

(1) Buyer will know whether seller has tendered conforming goods by inspecting the tender. See § 2-512 and § 2-513, previously discussed in this chapter, on inspection.

(2) Buyer always has the right to inspect the goods before buyer can be deemed to have accepted those goods. When the contract provides that price is due on delivery (a "C.O.D." or "cash on delivery transaction"), buyer's payment for the goods is not acceptance of the goods. Buyer is still afforded the opportunity to inspect, whether in accord with the contract's specifications or, if the contract is silent, within a reasonable time and in a reasonable place and manner, before buyer can be deemed to have accepted the goods. § 2-512 and § 2-513.

(3) When, having inspected, buyer determines that the goods are conforming, buyer must accept and pay for those goods. § 2-606.

(4) Sometimes, once seller has tendered buyer will decline to inspect, or fail to inspect in a timely manner. In those

instances, once the time for inspection has passed buyer will be deemed to have accepted the goods even when they are nonconforming. § 2-606.

(5) Buyer's acceptance can be manifested overtly, by words.

(6) Buyer's acceptance can also be manifested implicitly, by conduct. Notice that § 2-606 provides that acceptance occurs whenever buyer signifies to seller that the goods are conforming or that the goods are acceptable no matter their nonconformity. Sometimes, buyer's mere silence after the time for inspection has passed will be deemed acceptance. Other times, buyer may not have overtly signaled to seller that the goods are acceptable but, by his conduct, shows that they are. For example, buyer uses the goods.

(7) A buyer who fails to accomplish a proper rejection of nonconforming goods will be deemed to have accepted those goods. See § 2-601 to § 2-605, which are discussed later in this chapter.

(8) A buyer who has accepted the goods bears several consequences, set forth in the next section to be discussed, § 2-607.

Example 2: Acceptance

Hannah ordered a living room chair from Ikea Furniture Store. Once she assembled it she sees that it wobbles. Has she accepted?

No. Remember that a buyer has a right to inspect under § 2-513 before she can be deemed to have accepted under § 2-606. Here, a reasonable inspection could not occur, and the defect not detected, until the chair was assembled. Now that Hannah has discovered the problem, however, she must take care to repack the chair and set it aside in order to avoid any inference that she is using it or engaging in acts inconsistent with seller's ownership. She should promptly notify Ikea of the problem in accordance with their instructions for return of purchases.

The Consequences of Acceptance: § 2–607

§ 2-607: Effect of Acceptance

(1) The buyer must pay at the contract rate for any goods accepted.

(2) Acceptance of goods by the buyer precludes rejection of the goods accepted and if made with knowledge of a non-conformity cannot be revoked because of it unless the acceptance was based on the reasonable assumption that the non-conformity would be seasonably cured but acceptance does not of itself impair any other remedy provided by this Article for non-conformity.

(3) Where a tender has been accepted

(a) the buyer must within a reasonable time after he discovers or should have discovered any breach notify the seller of breach or be barred from any remedy.

(4) The burden is on the buyer to establish any breach with respect to the goods accepted.

The Context

Remember that a buyer has accepted goods under § 2-606 when he uses them or does any other act inconsistent with seller's ownership. Acceptance can also occur when the buyer waits too long before inspecting, only to then discover that there is a problem with the goods. Buyer will be deemed to have accepted when he fails to make an effective rejection. Acceptance has serious consequences for the buyer, as set forth in § 2-607. Those consequences are as significant as they are for several reasons. Most essentially, the presumption is that a buyer who has used the goods or otherwise signaled his acceptance either did so because they were in fact conforming or, if not now conforming, the problem with the goods is likely attributable to something that buyer did or did not do with respect to the goods.

Four Important Consequences of Acceptance

(1) Buyer must pay at the contract rate for any goods accepted, even when the goods are nonconforming.

(2) A buyer who has accepted goods loses the right to reject those goods. Acceptance and rejection are mutually exclusive. In other words, buyer cannot have it both ways. Buyer cannot signal (whether by words or sheer failure to object) that goods are suitable and then later successfully reject those goods. A buyer who has accepted non-conforming goods can try instead to revoke that acceptance under § 2-608, discussed in the next section, but cannot reject.

(3) A buyer who has accepted goods bears the burden of proving that the goods were nonconforming when tendered. (By contrast, when buyer rightfully rejects seller's tender because of the goods' nonconformity it is the seller who bears the burden of proving that the goods were conforming when tendered.) A buyer who has accepted goods and now alleges that those goods were nonconforming when tendered can sometimes face an insurmountable hurdle. The presumption is that the tender was conforming, hence prompting buyer's acceptance of the goods. Why else would buyer have accepted? Additionally, when a buyer who has accepted the goods only to later asserts that they are nonconforming must be prepared to rebut the inference that it was buyer who actually caused or

contributed to the problem now complained of. It is very difficult for buyer to rebut those presumptions.

(4) Perhaps most significantly, a buyer who is deemed to have accepted seller's tender must seasonably notify seller of the non-conformity **or be barred from any remedy**. Stated differently, a buyer who has accepted the goods must object (whether to their quality, quantity or for any other reason) in a timely manner or forever hold his piece. That is a very harsh and sometimes drastic consequence but a consequence of acceptance nonetheless. Hence, an attorney representing an aggrieved buyer is best advised to be alert to this potential consequence of her client's acceptance or run the risk of a later malpractice lawsuit.

Example 3: The Consequences of Acceptance

To prepare for her new job in Japan, Shoshanna orders a suitcase on wheels from Samsonite. The luggage arrives and Shoshanna uses it for a weekend road trip. The following week, as she tries out the luggage's wheels for the first time while at the airport, she finds the suitcase so difficult to pull that one of its wheels actually falls off. When she tries to return the suitcase, seller advises her that because it is used it cannot be returned. Advise Shoshanna.

Shoshanna accepted the suitcase under § 2-606. She used it twice, hence acting inconsistently with seller's ownership. She had the right to inspect before she could be deemed to have accepted. Here, it seems that she did not inspect in a sufficiently thorough manner. Had she done so, it appears that she would have discovered the difficulty with maneuvering the suitcase. Now that she has accepted, she bears the consequences set forth in § 2-607. She cannot reject (i.e., return) the suitcase under § 2-601. She could try to revoke under § 2-608, but that would depend on her demonstrating that the problem was a latent defect, as will be discussed next in this chapter. She must pay for the suitcase at the contract rate. She must promptly notify seller of the breach or be barred from any remedy for breach of warranty or other claim. Finally, because she accepted Shoshanna bears the burden of proving that the suitcase was nonconforming when tendered. That will be a daunting burden to satisfy, in view of the presumption that her use of the item contributed to or caused the problem that she now complains of.

A Buyer Who Accepts Cannot Reject but Can Try to Revoke That Acceptance: Revocation Under § 2–608

§ 2-608: Revocation of Acceptance in Whole or in Part

(1) The buyer may revoke his or her acceptance of a lot or commercial unit whose non-conformity substantially impairs its value to him or her if he or she has accepted it

(a) on the reasonable assumption that its non-conformity would be cured and it has not been seasonably cured; or

(b) without discovery of such non-conformity if his acceptance was reasonably induced either by the difficulty of discovery before acceptance or by the seller's assurances.

(2) Revocation of acceptance must occur within a reasonable time after the buyer discovers or should have discovered the ground for it and before any substantial change in condition of the goods which is not caused by their own defects. It is not effective until the buyer notifies the seller of it.

(3) A buyer who so revokes has the same rights and duties with regard to the goods involved as if he had rejected them.

The Context

A buyer who has accepted allegedly non-conforming goods can no longer reject those goods under § 2-601, but might, under certain circumstances, be able to revoke the acceptance. It is far more difficult to revoke an acceptance than it is to reject goods never accepted. The buyer who seeks to revoke must demonstrate that the problem complained of is more than slight and instead represents a substantial impairment in value to that buyer. Moreover, the buyer has to be able to explain why it is that he accepted the goods, in view of the nonconformity that he now alleges.

Revocation's Two Elements: Substantial Impairment in Value plus a Valid Justification for Buyer's Decision to Accept Nonconforming Goods

Unlike the more lenient standard for rejection, where a buyer who has not accepted the non-conforming goods is permitted to reject for any defect, however slight, successful revocation depends on buyer's demonstrating that the goods' defect(s) represents a substantial impairment in value to that buyer. The good news for an aggrieved buyer is that "substantial impairment in value" is defined subjectively. The Official Comments to § 2-608 provide that the relevant question is whether, because of the goods' nonconformity, *this buyer, in fact*, suffered a substantial impairment in value in view of the particular uses and purposes that this buyer intended for the goods. It does not matter that seller might not actually know or have reason to know of buyer's particular needs or intended purposes for the goods.

In addition to demonstrating that the nonconformity represents a substantial impairment in value, a buyer who has accepted non-conforming goods must provide a valid justification for the decision to accept. § 2-608 sets forth three circumstances that might justify buyer's acceptance of albeit nonconforming goods. First, buyer might have been duped into accepting based on seller's assurances that the defects would be cured, only to have seller renege on those assurances or otherwise fail to correct the defects. For example, buyer complains to seller of a problem with the goods and seller responds by promising to send a repairperson or a replacement only to then, after a significant time has elapsed, fail to do either.

Second, it might be that the defects were latent and did not manifest until acceptance had already occurred. For example, buyer purchased tulip bulbs that seemed fine, only to see months later that they failed to grow. Or perhaps buyer picks up his new car from the dealership, drives it for some distance and only then learns that the car's engine fails at speeds of 50 M.P.H. or more.

Third, it could be that buyer's acceptance was based on seller's vociferous assurances that there were no defects, so that those assurances essentially precluded buyer from inspecting as thoroughly as buyer had hoped. For example, when buyer arrives at the car dealership to pick up his brand new vehicle the dealer tells him, "*Go take this beauty out and enjoy the day. This car is perfect. I already checked out every nook and cranny. Stop obsessing and hit the open road! Now get out of here!*" That buyer may well have been precluded from inspecting as carefully as he would have but for the seller's assurances.

The Procedures for Revocation

A buyer who intends to revoke his or her acceptance must give seller notice of that intent within a reasonable time after buyer discovers or should have discovered the problem complained of. The Official Comments make plain that it is safest for buyer to act promptly and to particularize the basis for the alleged nonconformity to give seller a chance to cure (pursuant to § 2-508, discussed later in this chapter.) Certainly, buyer must act before the goods have undergone a substantial change in value not attributable to their defects.

Example 4: Revocation of Acceptance

Jessa purchased a sophisticated multi-lamp laser spotlight for her new business venture's premiere location. She needed one of the lamps to beam at a distance of 60 feet to be able to shine onto her adjacent location down the block. The spotlight arrived, Jessa set it up and it worked well for the opening night. The next night, however, the long-distance laser failed to operate. The rest of the spotlight is working well, but Jessa no longer wants it. Advise her on how best to proceed.

Jessa accepted the spotlight, under § 2-606, by using it. Therefore, she cannot reject under § 2-601, but she can try to revoke her acceptance under § 2-608. To revoke, she must first demonstrate that the defect that she complains of (one of the spotlight lamp's failure to beam at the needed distance) represents a substantial impairment in the good's value, as determined subjectively. She should be able to satisfy this first requirement for revocation in view of her particular needs and purposes for the goods. (Note here that it would be helpful to learn additional facts to know whether an implied warranty of fitness for a particular purpose under § 2-315 also applies). Second, she must provide a sufficient justification for her decision to accept this good whose defect constitutes a substantial impairment to her. Here, it may be that she can demonstrate that the defect now complained of was latent, and took some initial use before it would manifest. If so, she should have the right to revoke her acceptance.

When Goods Are Nonconforming and Seller Has Not Accepted, Buyer Is Within Its Rights to Reject the Tender: Rejection Under § 2–601

§ 2-601: Buyer's Rights on Improper Delivery

> Subject to the provisions of this Article on breach in installment contracts (§ 2-612) and unless otherwise agreed under the sections on contractual limitations of remedy (§ 2-718 and § 2-719), if the goods or the tender of delivery fail in any respect to conform to the contract, the buyer may
>
> (a) reject the whole; or
>
> (b) accept the whole; or
>
> (c) accept any commercial unit or units and reject the rest.

The Context

Suppose that seller tenders nonconforming goods. Buyer learns of the nonconformity as a result of buyer's inspection of those goods pursuant to § 2-513 and § 2-512, discussed earlier in this chapter. Buyer takes care to avoid accepting those defective goods, mindful of the expansive definition of acceptance set forth in § 2-606 and the adverse consequences of acceptance contained in § 2-607.

A buyer who has not yet accepted nonconforming goods is within its rights to reject the tender. Rejection, when accomplished properly, places buyer in the same remedial position as if seller never performed at all. (The range of remedies available to a buyer who properly rejects nonconforming goods will be discussed in the next chapter.)

Buyer Can Reject for Any Defect: "The Perfect Tender Rule"

§ 2-601 embraces the so-called "perfect tender rule" and makes rejection available for any nonconformity in quality or quantity, however slight. In other words, buyer has the right to demand a perfect tender from seller. Notice that the standard for rejection is far more generous to buyer than the standard that must be met for buyer to successfully revoke its acceptance under § 2-608.

Rejection Compared to Revocation

It is much more difficult for a buyer who has accepted goods to undo or revoke that acceptance on the basis of some nonconformity than it is for a buyer who never accepted the goods to reject a nonconforming tender. That is because a buyer who did after all accept the goods now alleged to be nonconforming must overcome the inference that the goods were conforming when tendered and suffered as a consequence of something that buyer did or failed to do. Unlike the more generous right to reject for any defect when buyer has not yet accepted the non-conforming goods, a buyer who has accepted goods that he now alleges to be non-conforming cannot revoke unless he can show that the nonconformity complained of represents a substantial impairment in value to him and that buyer's acceptance was basically duped because the goods' latent defects took time to manifest, seller promised to correct the problem but never did or seller's aggressive assurances or other diversionary tactics at the time and place for tender deprived buyer of the opportunity to inspect or to inspect as fully as he desired. *See* § 2-608.

Example 5: Rejection

Adam ordered 500 paint brushes for his new school for artists. When the shipment arrived he promptly inspected and saw that it was two brushes short. Advise Adam.

Adam has not accepted the goods under § 2-606. A buyer has the right to inspect under § 2-513, as long as exercised reasonably, before buyer will be deemed to have accepted. Since buyer has not accepted, he is within his rights to reject under § 2-601 and its perfect tender rule. A buyer may reject for any defect, however slight. Nonetheless, Adam should anticipate that seller may seek to cure by promptly tendering the missing brushes. Whether or not seller has the right to cure depends on application of § 2-508, discussed later in this chapter.

Procedures for Rightful Rejection: § 2–602 to § 2–605

§ 2-602: Manner and Effect of Rightful Rejection

(1) Rejection of goods must be within a reasonable time after their delivery or tender. It is ineffective unless the buyer seasonably notifies the seller.

(2) Subject to the provisions of the two following sections on rejected goods (§ 2-603 and § 2-604),

(a) after rejection any exercise of ownership by the buyer with respect to any commercial unit is wrongful as against the seller; and

(b) if the buyer has before rejection taken physical possession of goods in which he or she does not have a security interest under the provisions of this Article (subsection (3) of § 2-711), he or she is under a duty after rejection to hold them with

reasonable care at the seller's disposition for a time sufficient to permit the seller to remove them; but

(c) the buyer has no further obligations with regard to goods rightfully rejected.

(3) The seller's rights with respect to goods wrongfully rejected are governed by the provisions of this Article on seller's remedies in general (§ 2-703).

The Context

A buyer who seeks to reject because the tendered goods are non-conforming must follow the procedures for rightful rejection contained in § 2-602 to § 2-605. § 2-602 obliges buyer to reject within a reasonable time after delivery, and to provide prompt notification to seller that it is exercising its right to reject. Buyer has a duty after rejection to hold the goods for seller to retrieve.

When Rejecting, Buyer Must Particularize the Defects When They Are Curable: § 2–605

§ 2-605: Waiver of Buyer's Objections by Failure to Particularize

(1) The buyer's failure to state in connection with rejection a particular defect which is ascertainable by reasonable inspection precludes him or her from relying on the unstated defect to justify rejection or to establish breach

(a) where the seller could have cured it if stated seasonably; or

(b) between merchants when the seller has after rejection made a request in writing for a full and final written statement of all defects on which the buyer proposes to rely.

(2) Payment against documents made without reservation of rights precludes recovery of the payment for defects apparent in the documents.

Buyer Should Always Specify the Reasons for Rejection

§ 2-605 provides that buyer should always particularize the basis for her rejection whenever seller might be able to cure or correct the defect and whenever, between merchants, seller requests in writing a written statement of all defects. The takeaway here is that every buyer should endeavor to specify the nature of the problem that prompted the decision to reject. Otherwise, seller could claim that buyer's failure to particularize deprived seller of an opportunity to cure, under § 2-508, and that any damages that buyer might be entitled to ought to be set-off by the losses that could have been mitigated had seller been afforded the chance to do right by buyer.

The Merchant Buyer's Duties When Rejected Goods Are Perishable: § 2–603

§ 2-603: Merchant Buyer's Duties as to Rightfully Rejected Goods

(1) Subject to any security interest in the buyer (subsection (3) of § 2-711), when the seller has no agent or place of business at the market of rejection a merchant buyer is under a duty after rejection of goods in his or her possession or control to follow any reasonable instructions received from the seller with respect to the goods and in the absence of such

instructions to make reasonable efforts to sell them for the seller's account if they are perishable or threaten to decline in value speedily.

(2) When the buyer sells goods under subsection (1), he or she is entitled to reimbursement from the seller or out of the proceeds for reasonable expenses of caring for and selling them, and if the expenses include no selling commission then to such commission as is usual in the trade or if there is none to a reasonable sum not exceeding ten per cent on the gross proceeds.

(3) In complying with this section the buyer is held only to good faith and good faith conduct hereunder is neither acceptance nor conversion nor the basis of an action for damages.

The Extent of the Duty

When a merchant buyer is rejecting goods that are perishable or threaten to decline quickly in value (such as food products), and seller does not have a representative or place of business at the market of rejection, that merchant buyer is required to await seller's instructions as to how best to proceed with respect to those perishables. If seller fails to provide instructions, the merchant buyer must make reasonable efforts to sell the perishables on seller's behalf. Note that buyer need not succeed with that effort, but must at least make a good faith attempt at it. Buyer is able to recover expenses incurred as an incident of the resale effort as incidental damages under § 2-715.

Buyer's Duties upon Rejecting When Buyer Is Not a Merchant and/or the Rejected Goods Are Not Perishable: § 2–604

§ 2-604: Buyer's Options as to Salvage of Rightfully Rejected Goods

> Subject to the provisions of the immediately preceding section on perishables if the seller gives no instructions within a reasonable time after notification of rejection the buyer may store the rejected goods for the seller's account or reship them to him or her or resell them for the seller's account with reimbursement as provided in the preceding section. Such action is not acceptance or conversion.

The Extent of the Duty

When the rejected goods are not perishable or the rejected goods are perishable and buyer is not a merchant, buyer must promptly notify seller that it is rejecting and then buyer must await seller's instructions as to how best to proceed with the rejected goods. If seller does not provide those instructions within a reasonable time after receiving notice of buyer's rejection, buyer is within its rights to store or reship the goods or resell them on seller's behalf. Those actions would not constitute acceptance under § 2-606. Buyer is entitled to reimbursement for reasonable expenses incurred in storing, shipping or reselling, under § 2-715's provision on incidental damages.

A Summary of the Procedures for Rightful Rejection: § 2–602 to § 2–605 in Four Steps

(1) When seller's tender is nonconforming, buyer must give seller seasonable notice of his desire to reject the goods. § 2-602. What is or is not timely notice depends on what the contract

says and, in the absence of a contract provision on point, the parties' course of performance, course of dealing and industry custom (the triplets).

(2) In that notice buyer must specify the reasons for the rejection whenever the defect is curable or seller requests that buyer particularize the basis for its rejection. A buyer who fails to specify the basis for a curable nonconformity or who fails to provide specifics in response to seller's request for those loses the right to reject as well as the right to establish a breach of contract. § 2-605. The takeaway is that buyer should always specify the basis for rejection, whether buyer deems the defects curable or not and whether seller requests particularization or not, to close the door to seller's assertion that if it had only known of the grounds for rejection it could have done something to make things right for buyer and thereby preserve the essence of the deal.

(3) Once buyer gives timely notice of its desire to reject non-perishable goods on the basis of their nonconformity, buyer typically is obliged to await seller's instructions on what to do with the goods. If no instructions are forthcoming, § 2-604 allows buyer to store, ship or resell the goods on seller's behalf. The expenses of storage, shipment or resale are recoverable as part of buyer's incidental or out-of-pocket expenses occasioned by seller's breach. See § 2-715, discussed in chapter nine.

(4) When the nonconforming goods are perishable and buyer is a merchant, buyer must make reasonable efforts to resell the goods on seller's account if seller has no agent or place of business at the site of rejection. § 2-603 imposes this affirmative duty to mitigate only: i.) when the goods threaten to decline quickly in value (they are perishable); ii.) buyer is a merchant (and presumably familiar with the local market) and

iii.) seller would presumably have significant difficulty reselling in view of the exigencies of time and the disadvantages of being without an agent in the locale. Note that in those circumstances the merchant buyer must at least make a good faith attempt to resell on seller's behalf. Buyer is not obliged to succeed at that effort, but must at least try, unless the circumstances are such as to justify the conclusion that any such effort would be fruitless.

Example 6: Procedures for Rightful Rejection

Ray owns a coffee shop in Brooklyn. He orders 30 dozen sesame seed bagels from Einstein Bagels, a Pittsburgh company. Poppy seed bagels arrive instead. Ray detests poppy seeds and rejects the bagels He promptly reaches out to seller, who does not return his calls or e-mails. How should Ray proceed?

Ray has the right to reject the bagels for their nonconformity, pursuant to § 2-601. He complied with the duty to provide timely notice of his desire to reject under § 2-602. Hopefully he particularized the problem in accordance with § 2-605, to afford seller an opportunity to cure if possible under § 2-508. Now, assuming that seller does not have an agent or place of business in Brooklyn (a reasonable assumption given that the company is located in Pittsburgh), Ray as a merchant has a duty to make reasonable efforts to resell the bagels on Einstein's account. Perhaps he can sell them to a nearby vendor. Alternatively, he is best advised to bite the bullet and resell the bagels on Einstein's behalf. By doing that he mitigates his damages and will not suffer a set-off in any damages award based on the losses he could have cut had he promptly resold on Einstein's behalf.

Seller's Right to Cure: § 2–508

§ 2-508: Cure by Seller of Improper Tender or Delivery; Replacement

(1) Where any tender or delivery by the seller is rejected because non-conforming and the time for performance has not yet expired, the seller may seasonably notify the buyer of his or her intention to cure and may then within the contract time make a conforming delivery.

(2) Where the buyer rejects a non-conforming tender which the seller had reasonable grounds to believe would be acceptable with or without money allowance the seller may if he or she seasonably notifies the buyer have a further reasonable time to substitute a conforming tender.

The Context

Suppose that seller tenders nonconforming goods. Recall that if buyer has not yet accepted the goods he is within his rights to reject them. (*See* § 2-601 to § 2-605). If buyer has accepted, buyer cannot reject but, in certain circumstances, can revoke the acceptance. (*See* § 2-608). Whether buyer rightfully rejects the goods or revokes his acceptance of the goods, pursuant to § 2-508 seller may have the opportunity to cure or correct the problem(s) that buyer complains of.

§ 2-508 does not prescribe how cure is to be accomplished. The case law provides that seller can cure by tendering a conforming replacement or, if appropriate, by repairing the defect.

Seller's Right to Cure When the Time for Performance Has Not Yet Come Due

If the contractually-provided time for performance has not yet come due, seller has an unrestricted right to cure. In other words, when seller tenders delivery earlier than contractually specified and buyer rightfully rejects or revokes in response to the goods' defects seller is entitled to a second chance to get it right by tendering conforming goods by the time specified in the contract. Article 2 liberally assures that right in order to preserve the essence of the deal.

Seller's Right to Cure When the Time for Performance Has Come Due

When seller tenders nonconforming goods on the contract's due date, so that the time for performance has arrived, it does not enjoy an unfettered right to cure. Instead, seller may cure only if she had a reasonable basis for believing that the tender, albeit nonconforming, would nonetheless be acceptable to buyer. Seller would have those reasonable grounds when the problem complained of is so minor or slight that seller assumed that it would not be a problem. Hence, § 2-508 modifies the perfect tender rule imposed by § 2-601 (which gives buyer the right to reject nonconforming goods for any defect, however *de minimis*) and allows seller the right to correct minor defects. The idea here is that when the problem complained of is slight, seller should be able to correct it quickly and efficiently, thereby preserving the essence of the deal and avoiding a breach of contract suit.

Seller also has reasonable grounds to believe that the tender would be conforming when she sells from her stock of inventory. Most goods come in packages. It may well be that the defect that buyer complains of was not detectable on sight. Sellers are entitled to assume that the items on their shelves are suitable. When that assumption yields to fact, seller is given another chance to get it right.

Finally, sometimes the triplets (the parties' course of performance, course of dealing and trade usage) provide the basis for seller's reasonable belief that her tender, albeit nonconforming, would nonetheless be acceptable. For example, there might be an industry tolerance for deviations in quality or quantity that justified in seller the expectation that her tender, although not conforming to the letter of the contract's terms, conformed to the spirit of the deal and the parties' common basis for expectation. When buyer disabuses seller of that belief seller should be given the chance to remediate.

Example 7: Seller's Right to Cure

Elijah, a dancer, ordered tap shoes from Rialto Tap, delivery promised for Nov. 1. On Nov. 1, the shoes arrived. Elijah tried them on and one of the laces frayed. He promptly rejects. Does Rialto have a right to cure?

Yes. The time for performance has come due. Thus, Rialto is permitted to cure only if it had reasonable grounds to believe that the tender, while nonconforming, would nonetheless be acceptable to buyer. While Elijah is within his rights to reject for even this slight defect, here Rialto presumably had reasonable grounds to believe that the tender, with the easily replaceable frayed lace, would be acceptable. Hence, it should be given another opportunity to promptly cure, either by tendering new laces or new shoes.

CHAPTER 9

Buyer's Remedies for Seller's Breach of Contract: The 2-700s

An Overview

If seller has breached its performance obligations, buyer is within its rights to pursue a remedy. A host of circumstances can trigger buyer's entitlement to a remedy. For example, seller might fail to tender the goods contracted for, or fail to tender conforming goods on time. Alternatively, seller might repudiate before the time for performance comes due.

The Aggrieved Buyer's Range of Remedies

Buyer's remedial options are indexed in § 2-711 and then elaborated upon in various sections found in the 2-700s. Buyer's remedial options include:

- **The right to cancel** the contract, pursuant to § 2-711.

- **The return of any down payment** or deposit that buyer had remitted to seller, recoverable under § 2-711.
- **Cover**, available under § 2-712, which allows an aggrieved buyer without the goods contracted-for to procure a substitute on the open market.
- **Specific performance**, pursuant to § 2-716, available when the goods are unique or in "other proper circumstances," allows the court to compel the breaching seller to tender the contracted-for goods to buyer.
- **Money damages** under § 2-713, which award the buyer who is without the goods contracted-for the difference between market price and contract price at the time and place that buyer learns of the breach.
- **Money damages** under § 2-714, which awards the buyer who has accepted non-conforming goods either the difference between the value of the goods as warranted and their actual value in view of their defects or recovery for any loss resulting in the ordinary course from seller's breach.
- **Incidental and consequential damages**, available under § 2-715, to allow buyer to recover, in addition to its direct measure of recovery, any out-of-pocket losses or reasonably foreseeable consequential damages.

Buyer's Right to Cover: § 2–712

§ 2-712: "Cover"; Buyer's Procurement of Substitute Goods

(1) After a breach within the preceding section the buyer may "cover" by making in good faith and without unreasonable delay any reasonable purchase of or contract to purchase goods in substitution for those due from the seller.

(2) The buyer may recover from the seller as damages the difference between the cost of cover and the contract price together with any incidental or consequential damages as hereinafter defined (§ 2-715), but less expenses saved in consequence of the seller's breach.

(3) Failure of the buyer to effect cover within this section does not bar him from any other remedy.

The Context

Cover is available to an aggrieved buyer when seller has repudiated the contract, failed to deliver or tendered non-conforming goods, prompting buyer to rightfully reject or, when buyer has accepted, to properly revoke that acceptance. Cover allows the aggrieved buyer to go into the market to procure goods in substitution for those contracted-for. Cover is a viable option for the aggrieved buyer when she continues to have a need for the goods no matter seller's failure to perform properly and there is a reasonable commercial equivalent for the goods that is available on the open market.

The Measure of Damages for a Buyer Who Covers

The buyer who successfully covers is entitled to the difference between the contract price and cover price, together with any incidental and consequential damages. Typically, there will be a difference between the contract price and cover price. Seller likely failed to perform because, when the time for performance arrived, the market had shifted to seller's advantage, allowing seller to reap more for the goods on the open market than she would under the contract. The same market shift that favors seller works to the detriment of buyer. By awarding the buyer who covers the difference between the contract price and the market price, buyer is given the benefit of the bargain originally struck with the breaching seller.

How to Properly Cover

§ 2-712 provides that the buyer who covers need not procure goods identical to those contracted-for. Still, the substituted goods must be a reasonable commercial equivalent for those that were the subject matter of the contract. Buyer cannot use cover to unreasonably upgrade or otherwise exploit the opportunity to reap a windfall. Cover must be exercised in good faith.

Cover is not mandatory but, if a reasonable commercial equivalent for the goods contracted-for does exist, a buyer who declines the opportunity to cover will have his damages award reduced based on the losses that could have been avoided had he covered. Cover, at bottom, is intended to be a mitigation principle, available as a way for buyer to reduce rather than compound his losses.

Finally, cover as a remedial option is not limited to merchants. Official Comment 4 to § 2-712 provides that non-merchants can exercise the right to cover. Note, however, that a non-merchant is often at a considerable disadvantage when it comes to procuring a good that is more sophisticated or outside the norm. Do you see why? The difficulties that buyer might experience when attempting to cover can be a basis for an award of specific performance to the aggrieved buyer. *See* § 2-716, discussed later on in this chapter.

Example 1: Cover

Monica ordered Calphalon non-stick stainless steel pots for her new restaurant's kitchen, purchase price $14,000. Seller tendered the pots and on inspection Monica discovered that several were missing their handles. She promptly rejected and purchased Williams-Sonoma copper pots instead, purchase price $20,000. What is her measure of recovery from seller?

Seller tendered non-conforming goods. Monica was within her rights to reject them and then procure a commercially equivalent substitute on the open market. Pursuant to § 2-712, a buyer who covers properly is entitled to the difference between the contract price and cover price, together with any incidental and consequential damages under § 2-715. If the substituted pots are in fact a reasonable commercial equivalent for the pots contracted-for, Monica is entitled to $6,000 as her direct measure of recovery. Here, the relevant question is whether the copper pots are a commercial equivalent for the stainless steel pots. Buyer is not entitled to use cover as an opportunity to upgrade. If the substituted pots are not commercially equivalent to those contracted-for, Monica's measure of damages is the difference between market price and contract price at the time and place of breach.

Specific Performance: § 2–716

§ 2-716: Buyer's Right to Specific Performance

(1) Specific performance may be decreed where the goods are unique or in other proper circumstances.

(2) The decree for specific performance may include such terms and conditions as to payment of the price, damages, or other relief as the court may deem just.

(3) The buyer has a right of replevin for goods identified to the contract if after reasonable effort he is unable to effect cover for such goods or the circumstances reasonably indicate that such effort will be unavailing or if the goods have been shipped under reservation and satisfaction of the security interest in them has been made or tendered. In the case of goods bought for person, family, or household purposes, the buyer's right of replevin vests upon acquisition of a special property, even if the seller had not then repudiated or failed to deliver.

The Context

Sometimes, in equity, the court will be persuaded to decree that the breaching seller must tender the contracted-for goods to buyer. As you might imagine, courts tend to be reluctant to award specific performance because of the burdens that such a decree puts upon the judicial system. If seller fails to comply with the court's order, the matter will be back on the court's docket. To enforce its decree, the court may have to issue a contempt order against seller and compel the sheriff to recover the goods on buyer's behalf. Judges hope to avoid those impositions on often already-crowded dockets and overtaxed law enforcement agents. Hence, at common law, specific performance is considered an extraordinary remedy, available only when the goods are unique so that no substitute is available.

Article 2 liberalizes the common law standard for specific performance. § 2-716 provides that specific performance is available when the goods are unique or "in other proper circumstances." The buyer who succeeds in its suit for specific performance is also entitled to incidental or consequential damages under § 2-715.

Knowing When Goods Are "Unique" or "Other Proper Circumstances" Are Present

Goods are unique when they have been identified to the contract, distinguishable from the world of similarly situated goods and not capable of ready substitute. For example, works of art, rare coins and limited edition stamps are unique.

§ 2-716 also allows for the possibility of an award to buyer of specific performance in "other proper circumstances." The case law has found those proper circumstances when, although the goods are not unique, buyer has a significant degree of difficulty in covering. Specific performance has also been awarded when buyer, having contracted with seller for goods, enters into a contract to sell those goods to a third party. Seller's nonperformance renders buyer liable to that third party for breach of contract.

Example 2: Specific Performance

Ross, a paleontologist, contracts with Fossil Facsimile for the purchase of a replica T-rex skeleton. Ross will restore the replica and then is contractually bound to sell it to the Smithsonian. Fossil Facsimile failed to tender the skeleton. Advise Ross.

Ross has a claim for specific performance under § 2-716. First, the skeleton replica may be unique. More facts are needed to know that for sure. Second, even if not unique, the facts present the kind of "other proper circumstances" to form the basis for an award of specific performance. Ross will be liable to a third party, the Smithsonian, if Fossil Facsimile fails to perform.

Buyer's Right to Money Damages Under § 2–713

§ 2-713: Buyer's Damages for Non-delivery or Repudiation

(1) Subject to the provisions of this Article with respect to proof of market price (§ 2-723), the measure of damages for non-delivery or repudiation by the seller is the difference between the market price at the time when the buyer learned of the breach and the contract price together with any incidental and consequential damages provided in this Article (§ 2-715), but less expenses saved in consequence of the seller's breach.

(2) Market price is to be determined as of the place for tender or, in cases of rejection after arrival or revocation of acceptance, as of the place of arrival.

The Context

Suppose that seller has breached the contract by failing to tender conforming goods on time. It may be that the circumstances are such that buyer now no longer has a need or use for the goods. In that case, neither cover nor specific performance are helpful. Instead, the aggrieved buyer may elect to pursue money damages from the breaching seller. § 2-713 applies to give buyer the benefit of the bargain that was struck by awarding the buyer who is without the goods contracted-for the difference between the contract price and the market price at the time and place that buyer learns of the breach. In addition to that direct measure of recovery, buyer is entitled to incidental and consequential damages under § 2-715.

Money Damages Under § 2–714

§ 2-714: Buyer's Damages for Breach in Regard to Accepted Goods

(1) Where the buyer has accepted goods and given notification (subsection (3) of § 2-607) he may recover as damages for any non-conformity of tender the loss resulting in the ordinary course of events from the seller's breach as determined in any manner which is reasonable.

(2) The measure of damages for breach of warranty is the difference at the time and place of acceptance between the value of the goods accepted and the value they would have had if they had been as warranted, unless special circumstances show proximate damages of a different amount.

(3) In a proper case any incidental and consequential damages under the next section may also be recovered.

The Context

Sometimes, either intentionally or inadvertently, buyer accepts the goods contracted-for no matter their nonconformity. Recall that acceptance is defined in § 2-606. A buyer who has accepted the goods suffers consequences outlined in § 2-607 and discussed earlier. Significantly, § 2-607 provides that the buyer who has accepted must prove that the goods were nonconforming at the time and place of tender. It can be difficult to sustain that burden, particularly in the face of seller's likely assertion that buyer's use caused or contributed to the defects now complained of.

A buyer who accepts the goods loses the right to reject them under § 2-601 but might be able to revoke the acceptance under § 2-608. When revocation is unavailable or inapplicable, a buyer who has accepted non-conforming goods can pursue remedies under § 2-714. § 2-714(1) provides that buyer may recover for any losses resulting from seller's breach in the ordinary course. The statute is deliberately vague here, allowing for it to be applied malleably depending on the given facts and circumstances.

Applying § 2–714

Most often, the buyer who accepted non-conforming goods will pursue the remedy contained in § 2-714(2). That section applies when buyer has a claim for breach of warranty against seller. For example, perhaps the goods are not as expressly warranted (pursuant to § 2-313). Maybe they are not fit for their ordinary purposes and therefore betray the guarantees of the implied warranty of merchantability set forth in § 2-314. Perhaps seller knew or had reason to know of buyer's particular purposes for the goods, buyer relied on seller's judgment in selecting suitable goods and the goods are actually unfit for those purposes. In those cases, buyer will have a claim for breach of the implied warranty of fitness for a particular purpose under § 2-715.

§ 2-714(2) provides that in a successful claim for breach of warranty, buyer's damages are to be measured by the difference between the value of the goods as warranted and their value in view of their defects at the time and place of acceptance, plus any incidental or consequential damages under § 2-715. The goods' value as warranted is typically the contract price. The goods' value in their defective condition is usually considerably less than the contract price, and sometimes will be of no value.

Buyer's Incidental and Consequential Damages: § 2–715

§ 2-715: Buyer's Incidental and Consequential Damages

(1) Incidental damages resulting from the seller's breach include expenses reasonably incurred in inspection, receipt, transportation and care and custody of goods rightfully rejected, any commercially reasonable charges, expenses or commissions in connection with effecting cover and any other reasonable expense incident to the delay or other breach.

(2) Consequential damages resulting from the seller's breach include

(a) any loss resulting from general or particular requirements and needs of which the seller at the time of contracting had reason to know and which could not reasonably be prevented by cover or otherwise; and

(b) injury to person or property proximately resulting from any breach of warranty.

The Context

In addition to its direct measure of recovery, an aggrieved buyer is within its rights under § 2-715 to pursue recovery for any incidental and consequential losses occasioned by seller's breach.

Defining Incidental Damages

Incidental damages are those out-of-pocket expenses that buyer incurred as a result of seller's failure to perform properly. Those out-of-pocket or administrative costs might include:

- Reasonable expenses incurred by buyer in rejecting the goods (under § 2-601 to § 2-605) or revoking any acceptance of nonconforming goods (under § 2-608), such as storage costs or shipping costs.
- Reasonable expenses incurred by covering or procuring goods in substitution for the goods contracted-for under § 2-712, such as search fees and travel costs.
- Costs of inspection under § 2-513.
- Reasonable attorneys' fees.

Defining Consequential Damages

Consequential damages are compensable for any loss sustained by buyer as a reasonably foreseeable consequence of seller's breach. Those might include buyer's lost profits or any other predictable losses suffered as a result of buyer's lost opportunity to put seller's performance to its intended purpose.

CHAPTER 10

Seller's Remedies

An Overview

Seller has a number of remedies available to it when buyer fails to perform. Buyer could betray her performance obligations by, for example, failing to pay for conforming goods, wrongfully repudiating, wrongfully rejecting the goods or wrongfully revoking her acceptance of the goods. Just as § 2-711 catalogues buyer's remedial options, § 2-703 provides the menu of seller's remedial rights.

The Aggrieved Seller's Range of Remedies

A seller confronted with buyer's nonperformance can:

- **Cancel the contract** under § 2-703(f)
- **Resell** the goods on the breaching buyer's account under § 2-706
- Sometimes **recover the contract price** in an action for the price under § 2-709
- **Recover money damages** under § 2-708

- **Recover for incidental and consequential damages** under § 2-710
- Add to this analysis consideration of whether the parties, in their contract, modified, displaced or limited any of the remedial entitlements otherwise assured by Article 2. § 2-719 allows for that possibility, subject to unconscionability doctrine.

Resale: § 2–706

§ 2-706: Seller's Resale Including Contract for Resale

(1) Under the conditions stated in § 2-703 on seller's remedies, the seller may resell the goods concerned or the undelivered balance thereof. Where the resale is made in good faith and in a commercially reasonable manner the seller may recover the difference between the resale price and the contract price together with any incidental damages allowed under the provisions of this Article (§ 2-710), but less expenses saved in consequence of the buyer's breach.

(2) Except as otherwise provided in subsection (3) or unless otherwise agreed resale may be at public or private sale including sale by way of one or more contracts to sell or of identification to an existing contract of the seller. Sale may be as a unit or in parcels and at any time and place and on any terms but every aspect of the sale including the method, manner, time, place and terms must be commercially reasonable. The resale must be reasonably identified as referring to the broken contract, but it is not necessary that the goods be in existence or that any or all of them have been identified to the contract before the breach.

(3) Where the resale is at private sale the seller must give the buyer reasonable notification of his intention to resell.

(4) Where the resale is at public sale

(a) only identified goods can be sold except where there is a recognized market for a public sale of futures in goods of the kind; and

(b) it must be made at a usual place or market for public sale if one is reasonably available and except in the case of goods which are perishable or threaten to decline in value speedily the seller must give the buyer reasonable notice of the time and place of the resale; and

(c) if the goods are not to be within the view of those attending the sale the notification of sale must state the place where the goods are located and provide for their reasonable inspection by prospective bidders; and

(d) the seller may buy.

(5) A purchaser who buys in good faith at a resale takes the goods free of any rights of the original buyer even though the seller fails to comply with one or more of the requirements of this section.

(6) The seller is not accountable to the buyer for any profit made on any resale. A person in the position of a seller (§ 2-707) or a buyer who has rightfully rejected or justifiably revoked acceptance must account for any excess over the amount of his security interest, as hereinafter defined (subsection (3) of § 2-711).

When It Applies

A seller who still has the goods contracted-for, whether because buyer wrongfully cancelled or repudiated the contract, wrongfully rejected or revoked acceptance of the goods is within its rights to resell those goods on the breaching buyer's behalf. It is important to note that resale is an option and not a mandate for the aggrieved seller.

Resale on seller's side is analogous to cover on buyer's side. Recall that cover, prescribed by § 2-712, allows buyer to procure goods in substitution for those seller fails to deliver properly, entitling buyer to recover the difference between the contract price and the cover price. Resale allows the aggrieved seller, now stuck with the goods buyer wrongfully refuses to accept, to resell them and recover the difference between contract price and resale price. Like cover on buyer's side, seller's right to resell is meant to afford seller the opportunity to mitigate or cut its losses. While seller is not required to resell on the defaulting buyer's behalf, a seller who declines to do so when resale could have spared seller some of its losses may suffer a set-off or reduction in its damages award.

How to Properly Resell

A seller who chooses to resell the goods contracted-for must accomplish the resale in good faith and in a commercially reasonable manner. What is or is not reasonable will depend on the totality of the surrounding circumstances and will be informed by the parties' course of performance, course of dealing and trade usage (the triplets).

Seller gets to decide whether the resale will be private or by public auction. If private, seller must give buyer notice of its intent to resell. If by public auction, the resale must take place at the customary place or market when one is reasonably available. When the goods are perishable or threaten to decline quickly in value, seller must give buyer reasonable notice of the time and place of the resale.

The Measure of Damages for the Seller Who Resells

A seller who successfully resells is entitled to the difference between the contract price and the resale price, plus any incidental or consequential damages under § 2-710. Often, there will be a difference between those two metrics. Buyer may have walked away from the contract because of a post-contract market shift that renders the market price for the goods contracted-for considerably less than the contract price. The same market shift that redounds to buyer's advantage will render it likely that seller will experience a shortfall when it resells those goods to a third party.

Seller's Action for the Price: § 2–709

§ 2-709: Action for the Price

(1) When the buyer fails to pay the price as it becomes due the seller may recover, together with any incidental damages under the next section, the price

(a) of goods accepted or of conforming goods lost or damaged within a commercially reasonable time after risk of their loss has passed to the buyer; and

(b) of goods identified to the contract if the seller is unable after reasonable effort to resell them at a reasonable price or the circumstances reasonably indicate that such effort will be unavailing.

(2) Where the seller sues for the price he must hold for the buyer any goods which have been identified to the contract and are still in his control except that if resale

becomes possible he may resell them at any time prior to the collection of the judgment. The net proceeds of any such resale must be credited to the buyer and payment of the judgment entitles him to any goods not resold.

(3) **After the buyer has wrongfully rejected or revoked acceptance of the goods or has failed to make a payment due or has repudiated (§ 2-610), a seller who is held not entitled to the price under this section shall nevertheless be awarded damages for non-acceptance under the preceding section.**

When It Applies

When buyer wrongfully rejects, revokes or repudiates, so that seller has the conforming goods contracted-for, sometimes that aggrieved seller will be entitled to recover the contract price from the breaching buyer. Seller, in turn, tenders the goods to buyer. Seller's action for the price is analogous to buyer's action for specific performance under § 2-716. Whereas specific performance has the court ordering that seller come forth with the goods that are the subject matter of the contract, an action for the price has the court decreeing that buyer must remit the purchase price for the goods and in turn presumably accept those goods that it paid for.

How It Works

Like specific performance on buyer's side, seller's action for the price is out of the norm and dependent for its success on several predicates. First, seller's action for the price is deemed premature until the time for payment has come due and buyer has failed to pay. Seller does not have an anticipatory right to the price.

Second, once the time for payment has come due and buyer has not paid, seller's action for the contract price will reside only if one of three circumstances is present. Either:

- Buyer accepted the goods under § 2-606 and failed to pay for them.
- The risk of loss of conforming goods had passed to buyer and the goods are damaged or destroyed thereafter. Recall that § 2-509 indicates how and when the risk of loss passes from seller to buyer. Once that risk has passed, any damage or devastation to the goods is buyer's problem (hopefully buyer has insurance) and buyer is obliged to pay for the goods at the contract rate.
- Buyer wrongfully refused conforming goods and seller is unable to resell those goods under § 2-706 after a reasonable attempt to do so or seller can show that under the circumstances any attempt to resell would be futile. When goods are customized, quickly perishable or specially manufactured for buyer, often seller will not be able to resell those goods on buyer's behalf. Similarly, a good that suffers obsolescence shortly after buyer's breach will be difficult for seller to resell.

A seller who succeeds with an action for the price is also entitled to recovery for its incidental and consequential losses under § 2-710.

Example 1: Seller's Action for the Price

Rachel orders customized wedding invitations from Galleria Stationers. The invitations are to be delivered to Rachel on Nov. 1 at a price of $1,200. On Oct. 15, after Galleria made a substantial beginning in performance, Rachel called to say that she no longer wanted the invitations. Advise Galleria.

Galleria should have an action for the price under § 2-709 as of Nov. 1, when the time for performance comes due. The goods are specially manufactured for Rachel and not suitable for sale to others in the ordinary course of business.

Example 2: Seller's Action for the Price

Phoebe, owner of a New York folk music store and restaurant, orders customized menus from Galleria Stationers, a Maine-based company. The contract states that it is F.O.B. Maine. Galleria Stationers places conforming goods with the carrier. When they arrive, the box is badly dented and frayed. Phoebe opens the box and sees that the invitations are ruined, apparently by some sort of water damage. She refuses to pay for them. Advise Galleria.

Galleria should have an action for the price once the price comes due. This is a shipment contract (see chapter six). Thus, the risk of loss passed from seller to buyer once conforming goods were placed with the carrier. Phoebe should proceed against her own insurance provider for the damages. Still, she is liable to Galleria for the purchase price.

Seller's Right to Money Damages: § 2–708

§ 2-708: Seller's Damages for Non-Acceptance or Repudiation

(1) Subject to subsection (2) and to the provisions of this Article with respect to proof of market price (§ 2-723), the measure of damages for non-acceptance or repudiation by the buyer is the difference between the market price at the time and place for tender and the unpaid contract price together with any incidental

damages provided in this Article (§ 2-710), but less expenses saved in consequence of the buyer's breach.

(2) If the measure of damages provided in subsection (1) is inadequate to put the seller in as good a position as performance would have done then the measure of damages is the profit (including reasonable overhead) which the seller would have made from full performance by the buyer, together with any incidental damages provided in this Article (§ 2-710), due allowance for costs reasonably incurred and due credit for payments or proceeds of resale.

When It Applies

§ 2-708 sets forth the customary measure of money damages available to a seller who seeks redress for buyer's failure to perform and does not or cannot resell the goods contracted-for under § 2-706 and does not have an action for the price under § 2-709. Ordinarily, under § 2-708(1), the aggrieved seller is entitled to the difference between the contract price and the market price at the time and place of tender, plus any incidental or consequential losses under § 2-710. Note that there is apt to be a difference between those two metrics, mindful that a market shift in buyer's favor might have precipitated buyer's breach. The same market shift that favors buyer will work to seller's detriment. Seller nonetheless is entitled to the benefit of its bargain.

The Lost Volume Seller: § 2–708(2)

§ 2-708(2) applies when the direct measure of recovery prescribed by § 2-708(1) is inadequate, typically because the aggrieved seller is a "lost volume seller." When seller has a seemingly inexhaustible supply of goods that are the subject matter of this contract, so that buyer's breach is not the necessary predicate to seller's resale, the measure of damages permitted under § 2-706 will not make seller whole. Instead, because of buyer's breach, seller has suffered lost profits. Those are recoverable under § 2-708(2).

Example 3: Seller's Right to Money Damages

Bob, owner of a local radio shack, contracts with Chief Hopper for the sale of a high-end satellite radio, purchase price $2,000. Chief Hopper wrongfully rejects the radio. What is Bob's measure of recovery?

Bob is entitled to the benefit of the bargain, which would award him the difference between the contract price and the market price at the time and place of the breach, together with any incidental damages under § 2-710.

Example 4: The Lost Volume Seller

Bob, owner of a chain of Radio Shacks throughout the country, has a vast supply of radios. Chief Hopper contracted with Bob for the purchase of two dozen radios for $2,400 and then improperly rejected them. Bob sold the radios to Joyce for $2,300. What is Bob's measure of damages?

The resale measure of damages under § 2-706 would give Bob the difference between the contract price and resale price, $100. That differential will be inadequate when, given his seemingly limitless supply of radios, Bob could have sold two dozen radios to Joyce irrespective of Chief Hopper's breach. In other words, had Chief Hopper performed Bob would have closed two deals instead of just one. In those instances, § 2-708(2) awards Bob his lost profits. Official Comment 2 to § 2-708 states that "profit" is the "list price minus the cost to manufacturer" or the "list price minus cost to the dealer."

Seller's Incidental and Consequential Losses: § 2–710

§ 2-710: Seller's Incidental Damages

> Incidental damages to an aggrieved seller include any commercially reasonable charges, expenses or commissions incurred in stopping delivery, in the transportation, care and custody of goods after the buyer's breach, in connection with return or resale of the goods or otherwise resulting from the breach.

The Context

§ 2-710 specifically provides that in addition to its direct measure of recovery (whether under the § 2-706 resale formula, an award of the contract price under § 2-709 or money damages under § 2-708), an aggrieved seller is entitled to recover from the breaching buyer any out-of-pocket costs incurred as a reasonable incident of buyer's breach. Those could include search costs to find a substitute buyer, shipping costs and reasonable attorneys' fees.

§ 2-710 does not specifically provide for the aggrieved seller to recover consequential damages, or those reasonably foreseeable losses suffered by seller as a consequence of buyer's breach. Nonetheless, the case law has demonstrated a willingness to award those when seller can demonstrate, for example, that it suffered quantifiable loss of goodwill or lost or foregone opportunities as a reasonable consequence of buyer's breach.

Example 5: Seller's Incidental and Consequential Losses

Bob, owner of Radio Shack, contracts with Joyce for the sale of a high frequency radio able to transmit into space. He is excited about this sale because Joyce's home has garnered significant media attention for its alleged capabilities to connect with extraterritorial beings. The agreed upon purchase price is $3,500. Later, Joyce wrongfully cancels the contract. After a considerable search, Bob is able to find another buyer for the radio, a science lab at Cal Tech, and resells it for $3,000. What is Bob's measure of recovery?

First, Bob is entitled to his direct measure of damages, which is the difference between the contract price and resale price under § 2-706. That amount is $500. In addition, Bob is entitled to recovery for incidental losses, including the search costs in finding a substitute buyer and reasonable attorney fees. He could also be entitled to recovery for any consequential losses suffered as a reasonably foreseeable consequence of Joyce's breach. For example, perhaps Bob has suffered a quantifiable loss of notoriety or goodwill as a consequence of losing this highly publicized deal. Perhaps Bob can quantify the opportunities lost now that he can no longer use the status that would have been attributable to his providing Joyce with the radio that made such ground-breaking contact.

CHAPTER 11

Putting It All Together: Article 2 Review and Problems

Set forth below is a methodology for successfully synthesizing and analyzing Article 2 contracts for the sale of goods.

- First, whether on a law school exam, the bar exam or in practice, begin by determining whether Article 2 apples to the given transaction. Article 2 applies to contracts for the sale of goods. "Goods," as defined by § 2-105, are all things movable. A "sale" of goods under § 2-106 involves the passing of title to those goods from seller to buyer in exchange for a price.

- If the transaction is within Article 2's scope, analyze its given facts in accordance with these four tiers of analysis: first, was a valid contract formed, in accordance with the requirements set forth in the 2-200s of Article 2? Second, if a valid contract was formed, what is the content of that contract? Go primarily to the 2-300s to determine the deal's content. Third, have the parties satisfied their respective performance obligations? Those are contained in the 2-500s and 2-600s. Fourth, if buyer or seller has failed to perform properly and is in breach of contract, which remedial entitlements apply? Buyer and seller remedies are contained in the 2-700s.

- A checklist for the first tier of analysis: formation of the contract (the 2-200s):
  - Was an offer for the purchase or sale of goods made?
  - Does that offer qualify as a "firm offer" so that § 2-205 applies?
  - Has there been an appropriate acceptance of the offer under § 2-206?
  - Do the terms of the offer and terms of the assent fail to match up so that there is a "battle of the forms?" If so, go to § 2-207 to assess whether a contract has been formed nonetheless and, if it has, what to do with the variant terms.
  - Does the deal have to be authenticated by an appropriate writing under § 2-201's statute of frauds? If so, is there an appropriate writing that binds the party against whom enforcement is now sought? If not, do any of the exceptions to the statute of frauds apply?
  - Is the deal contained in a final writing that one of the parties now seeks to supplement or contradict as a consequence of some alleged sidebar understanding reached by the parties

before or at the time that this deal is formed? If so, turn to § 2-202 and the parol evidence rule.

    - Does a party to the contract allege a post-formation change in the deal's forms? If so, apply § 2-209 on contract modification.

- A checklist for the second tier of analysis: content of the contract (the 2-300s):
    - Have the parties expressly agreed on all terms? If so, their express terms control.
    - If there are gaps or missing terms in the agreement, did the parties intend to close the deal with finality nonetheless? Only if the answer is yes, proceed to the parties' course of performance, course of dealing and trade usage (the triplets), in that order to supply the missing term or terms. If the triplets are unavailing, turn to Article 2's gap-filler provisions, contained in § 2-305 to § 2-311.
    - Be sure to be able to identify both requirements, output and exclusive dealing contracts for the sale of goods, and the standards that apply to each under § 2-306.
    - To determine the quality of the goods contracted for, consult the contract's express terms in conjunction with Article 2's sections on warranties. The contract's express description of the goods, for example, creates an express warranty under § 2-313. Express warranties can also be found in the affirmations of fact that seller makes when those

statements form part of the basis of the bargain struck. Express warranties also include any blueprint or technical specifications that seller provides about the goods. When seller is a merchant, she impliedly promises that the goods are merchantable, or suitable for their ordinary purposes under § 2-314. When seller knows of buyer's particular needs for a good and that buyer is relying on seller's judgment to select the good suitable for those needs, the implied warranty of fitness for a particular purpose under § 2-315 provides that the goods must be suitable for those specialized needs. When applying warranties analysis to supply information about what it is that seller promised, whether explicitly or implicitly, about the goods' quality, take a cumulative approach under § 2-317. More than one warranty is likely to apply to the given facts. Remember to assess whether any warranties have been effectively disclaimed or modified under § 2-316. When a remote buyer suffers harm as a proximate cause of the goods' betrayal of promised quality standards, apply § 2-318 on privity together with supplemental principles of common law, such as products liability law.

- When an unforeseen contingency or calamity renders seller's performance impossible or impracticable, the parties' contract is apt to be silent on how the parties are to proceed. In those cases, turn to Article 2's sections on excuse doctrine to determine whether seller will be released or discharged from its contractual obligations. Impossibility of performance is treated in § 2-613 and impracticability in § 2-615. Integrate § 2-509 here to ascertain when the risk of loss passed from seller to buyer, and § 2-614 to determine the protocol for a claim of excuse.

- A checklist for the third tier of analysis: performance of the contract (the 2-500s and 2-600s):
  - Under § 2-503, seller performs by tendering the right goods to the right place at the right time and buyer performs by remitting the contracted-for price for the goods.
  - To ascertain whether seller has satisfied its performance obligation, buyer is afforded the opportunity to inspect the goods under § 2-512 and 2-513 prior to its being deemed to have accepted them under § 2-606.
  - To know buyer's entitlements when the goods are nonconforming, first determine whether or not buyer has already accepted the goods under § 2-606.
  - If buyer has not accepted the goods under § 2-606, buyer is within its rights to reject them for any defect, however slight, as long as it comports with the protocol for rightful rejection contained in § 2-601 to § 2-605.
  - If buyer has accepted the goods under § 2-606, buyer can try to revoke that acceptance under § 2-608 only if the problem complained of represents a substantial impairment in value to

the buyer and the circumstances are such that buyer's acceptance of the nonconforming goods is justifiable.

- Whether buyer rightfully rejects or revokes, consider whether seller is entitled to exercise its right to cure the defects that seller complains of under § 2-508.

- A checklist for the fourth tier of analysis: remedies (the 2-700s):
    - Buyer's remedies for seller's breach are indexed in § 2-703 and include cancellation, refund of any down payment or deposit, cover under § 2-712, money damages under § 2-713 and specific performance under § 2-716. Add to buyer's direct measure of recovery any incidental or consequential losses suffered under § 2-715.
    - Seller's remedies for buyer's breach are indexed in § 2-711 and include cancellation, resale under § 2-706, an action for the price under § 2-709 and money damages under § 2-710. Add to seller's direct measure of recovery any incidental or consequential losses suffered under § 2-710.
    - Keep in mind that the parties' remedial entitlements may be modified in the contract, an allowable exercise of freedom of contract under § 2-719, subject to unconscionability doctrine under § 2-302.

CHAPTER 12

On Grades

The ways that law schools test and evaluate students leaves much to be desired. In a context where traditionally there is so little feedback, how one happens to do on a particular day on a three or four hour exam takes on an undeserved importance and magnitude. Some even construe their grades as the final word on their abilities and opportunities. Nothing could be further from the truth.

Your grades, whatever they happen to be, are an indication of how well you fared for a few hours in applying your learning to a narrow, often peculiar format, as determined by someone else's sometimes arbitrary, usually subjective judgment. In this imperfect system, injustices are inevitable. People who studied hard may not do as well as they should or could have. People who hardly studied may excel. The course that you thought you aced becomes your worst grade. The exam that you thought you bombed comes back as your best grade. And so on.

Let your grades inform your life, not define, diminish or even exalt it. They are a means of feedback, letting you know whether you have figured out how to play the exam-taking game. If your grades aren't what they should be, take the offensive, seeking out people and resources to help you to improve your exam skills. Consult with each of your teachers. Find a tutor. Speak with students who have done well in the given courses you are now preparing for. Take practice exams. Ask your teachers for feedback on your practice runs.

For that matter, you have the power to dilute the significance of grades by demonstrating your excellence in other contexts. Whatever you do, be of service. The surest way out of your own struggles and pain is to help others out of theirs. Look around and wake up to the sea of need right in your midst. Then do what you can with the time and resources that you have. Do it for the sake of the constituencies that you help. Do it for your own sake. What you do for others you do for yourself. Then watch, as life rises up to meet you, doors open and the meaning that's been missing is found.

As you do everything you can to succeed in school and in life, try to keep matters in perspective. Remember that the race is long, and that to finish the race is to win the race. Pace yourself, and know that time is on your side. Be appreciative and grateful for the strides that you are making. Know that every step, however small, puts you that much closer to realizing your goal.

You are not your grades, or, for that matter, your standardized test scores, your resume or your summer job. Grades are simply information. They don't have the power to define you or limit the possibilities unless you give them that power. Don't. Do not surrender the song put in your heart to any teacher, employer, colleague or classmate. That song was put there for a reason, and it is yours alone to sing. The world needs your voice.

Only you create the reality that your grades represent. No one else. View them as an opportunity for learning, self-knowledge and growth. Throughout, keep your head high. Do not be cruel to yourself. Beyond a healthy discipline, be gentle with yourself. Hold tight to your dignity, integrity and belief in yourself. You are precisely where you should be. You have succeeded before. You are a success now.

Think, act and react as a successful, prosperous and intelligent person would. Remember that what you think about most expands. What you think about most is what you move towards. Success is more attitude than it is aptitude. With your thoughts and attitudes, you are writing your ticket.

CHAPTER 13

Five Guideposts for Assuring Success and Significance

Law school and the practice of law can cause even very self-assured people to have moments of doubt. These five guideposts will help you to build strength of purpose and motivation, particularly on those days when you find yourself questioning your abilities and your place in our craft.

(1) Know that you are smart enough to be here. If you are feeling intimidated, you are most likely presuming that your classmates are so much smarter than you, your teachers are all geniuses and the given material is so difficult that only the smartest people are able to understand it and work with it. All of that is nonsense and you need to get it out of your head right now.

Avoid any and all comparisons with others. What you bring to this pursuit is what only you can bring. The entire range of life experiences that led you to this moment are yours alone and they have prepared you well. Comparison is disrespect for yourself and the object of your comparative appraisal. It cannot help but have you thinking that you are *"more than"* or *"less than"* someone else.

That sort of conclusion is both presumptuous and false. Do not denigrate your unique aptitudes by comparing them to another's.

Moreover, your snap judgments about another's strengths or weaknesses are most likely wrong. Resist the urge to label people. Kierkegaard got it right when he said, "*If you label me, you negate me.*" Stop sizing up your classmates in some misguided attempt to determine where you stand. You are no better than and no worse than anyone else. Everyone has a story to tell and something to teach you. And you have your own story to tell, and something to teach the world.

When you start to feel overwhelmed or less than worthy, realize that you are most likely holding yourself to a crazy standard of perfection. Abandon the quest for some brand of nuanced excellence and simply commit to "good enough." As long as your performance in class, on the exam, on papers and other exercises is good enough you will be fine.

To finish the race is to win the race. You do not have to come in first, second or even in the top 99%. The last one to cross the finish line still crosses the finish line. Maintain a gentle discipline and cross the line.

(2) Declare right now that you love school. You might be thinking, "*But I don't.*" If so, change that perception now. Your life will meet you at your level of expectation and persistent rhetoric about it. What that means is, even if you have to fake it until you make it, you should begin, today, to enthusiastically declare your passion and admiration for everything about the education that you are receiving. Every day, state emphatically that you love school, your job and the people in your life. Sure enough and soon enough, reasons to be right about your declarations will start showing up. There is a force that meets good with good.

(3) **Arrive at your set of first principles.** It is important that you take some time to think about the virtues and values that matter most to you. Those are your first principles, meaning the code that you live by. They are the moral compass by which you chart your course and comport your behavior. They will help you to answer the most important question of all: *Who do you think you are?*

You will grow in power and stature as your daily habits comport with your first principles. Strive each day to keep your words and actions within your circle of core values. When you find yourself acting outside the circle, be self-corrective. Apologize, make amends and forgive yourself. Make the adjustments that you need to make to get back to center and then move forward.

To set your moral compass, finish these sentences *"These are the central values on which I base my life: ___________"* *"These are the attributes I admire most: __________________"* *"This is how I hope others would describe me: ____________"* Write down the answers on an index card. Use that card as a bookmark when you read. Refer to it often. It will help you to keep your head on straight, especially when others seem to be losing theirs. We suffer when we stray from our first principles. We find relief when we return to them.

I did that exercise before I began law school. I jotted down the answers on an index card, and I kept that card on my bulletin board, where I would see it every day. On that card, here is what I wrote:

> ***"I value intelligence and I respect kindness even more. I stand for the realization of equal access to justice for all. I believe in the promise of redemption and the power of love. I admire the relentless commitment to excellence when it is practiced with compassion. I seek to emulate those who stay above the fray, whose high-mindedness has no room for the***

petty or mean-spirited. I want to be remembered for seeing the good in everyone, because it is there."

Stay away from the bottom-feeders and traffickers in human frailties. Stay above the fray. When using the internet, do not let the anonymity of a comments section entice you to write something that is simply not worthy of you. Use social media responsibly. Let your digitized imprint be principled, generous and positive. Proclaim what you are ***for*** instead of decrying what you are ***against***. Take a stand for decency, fairness and the cause of justice. Stand on the side of virtue. Stick up for the underdog. Be a voice for someone who has yet to find his or her own. In the presence of cruelty, do not be impartial. There is a well of courage inside of you that you have not even begun to tap. Go to that well and draw from it. Speak your peace truthfully and with dignity, *but speak your peace*. To remain neutral in the presence of injustice is to stand for nothing. Complacency is the enemy of the good.

(4) Be mindful of the power of your words. Starting now, make sure that you do what you say you are going to do and that you do not do what you promise you won't do. Let your words advance the cause of progress. Be generous in your estimations of others. Eventually, people will meet you at your level of expectation for them. Centuries ago, the German philosopher Goethe got it right when he observed, *"If you treat an individual as he is, he will remain how he is. But if you treat him as if he were what he ought to be and could be, he will become what he ought to be and could be."*

Whenever you think a good or positive thought about another, say it out loud. If you think that a classmate made an excellent point in class, tell her. If you admire the statesmanship of a student leader on campus, tell him. If you strive to emulate the example of a particularly generous friend, tell her. If you are on the bus and you notice that the driver greets every passenger with courtesy and respect, compliment the driver. If a salesperson is doing a great job under pressure, say so out loud. There is so much that is negative and toxic out there in the marketplace of ideas. Do not leave the high-minded and positive observations unsaid.

Clean up your social media accounts. Right now, go through your Facebook, Twitter, Instagram, Snapchat and Tumblr accounts and delete any photographs, posts or other communications that would place you in a bad light. Revisit the internet addresses that you have ascribed to your on-line accounts. Make sure that they are professional. Prospective employers, graduate school admissions officers, current employers, potential clients, actual clients, co-workers, colleagues and countless others will be checking your virtual footprint before making decisions that could affect your life. In these new media times of ever-intersecting circles of influence and exchange, the personal cannot help but inform the professional. Take charge of the impression that your digitized patterns create.

Keep every communication to your professors, classmates, employers, co-workers and colleagues professional and high-minded. Never hit *send* in anger. Expect that every electronic submission that you send can and often will be forwarded to others, including unintended recipients. When you communicate with a professor, employer or colleague by e-mail, keep the tone respectful and professional. If you have to miss a class, write in advance, explain and apologize. In class, if you are confused about some part of the subject matter, say so clearly but also with humility and deference. For example, state, *"I am so sorry to bother you with this, but I am having the hardest time understanding Bentham's central thesis. Here is what I think he is suggesting ________________. Am I correct in that understanding?"*

Avoid colloquialisms and an informal tone. Do not place the burden of your confusion on your professor when you write asking for help or clarification. For example, do not write, *"For the life of me I just don't get what we did in class today. Maybe you could explain it again in class tomorrow?"* Instead, try, *"As I review my notes, there are a few points that I'm afraid I don't have down yet. Would it be ok if I came by office hours later this week?"*

(5) Be of service in all settings. Make every context in which you find yourself less about you and more about how you can be of service. Seek out ways to help. At the start of each day, declare that your intention is to make another's load lighter. Leave your ego at the door of every room that you are about to enter, and generously do something so that the room is better because you were there. That might mean mopping the floor or speaking kind words, adding clarity where there was confusion, baking for someone or making someone laugh. No matter the form that it takes, be of service.

Decide now that wherever your professional path takes you, you will use your expertise to ease the suffering of others. Keep that as your aim, and the opportunities to serve will find you. There is much to be done. Too many are without even a place to live. As I write these words, there are countless schoolchildren unable to concentrate because they are hungry. Others will never see the inside of a classroom.

In the midst of rising seas of need, you will do what you can with the time that you have. And that will make all the difference. Your virtue and commitment to social and economic justice will shake people out of their cynicism and despair and make them question whether they are right about their harsh judgments of the world. ***When people try to convict humanity, you will be their basis for reasonable doubt.***

Most of all, your assiduous commitment to the good of others will make your life beautiful. *You will be a witness to the birth of hope.* As a lawyer, I have had the privilege to watch as hope has sprung from the most desolate places. My life has never been the same.